1.25

Cash in the City

Cash in the City

Affording Manolos, Martinis, and Manicures on a Working Girl's Salary

Juliette Fairley

JOHN WILEY & SONS, INC.

ISBN 0-471-20981-3

Printed in the United States of America.

10 9 8 7 6 5 4 3 2 1

All glory to God

Contents

Foreword

So, you like living the sweet life. We hear you. We respect you.

You like to spend weekends in Nantucket. You're a fan of the Brazilian bikini wax. You love Cosabella thongs, dining out, and all the savvy missives you've found on the ultimate insiders' guide, *www.DailyCandy.com*.

But what are you doing about your finances?

Being a hip, fashionable sex kitten isn't cheap these days. While keeping up with the Joneses, have you skipped three meals because you were holding out for the Prada sample sale?

Though it's based on the principles of living the good life and indulging yourself, DailyCandy.com doesn't want to bankrupt you. As the founder of the coveted free daily e-mail that keeps everyone plugged in, I encourage you to read *Cash in the City: Affording Martinis, Manolos, and Manicures on a Working Girl's Salary*.

Juliette Fairley provides a how-to personal finance book for hip young city girls who marvel at how Carrie, Samantha, Miranda, and Charlotte on *Sex and the City* can look like a million bucks, live in those fabulous apartments, and not look like something the cat dragged in after an honest day's work. (Cheat sheet answer: That's television, baby, not reality!)

This book will help you to figure out how to do and have it all on a working girl's salary, encouraging you not to put your life on hold by giving tips on how to afford a vacation, start an investment club, decorate your home on a budget, and move up the ladder in corporate America. *Cash in the City* provides nitty-gritty details that you can't find in other personal finance books for women. Chapter 6, the beauty chapter, gives the names and addresses of shops in major cities where you can find designer clothes at a discount. And if working "for the man" (i.e., punching the clock and having someone else reap the benefits of all your brilliant ideas) doesn't appeal to you, there's a chapter on how to start a business with contact information for women venture capitalists around the country.

Dig in your heels, sign up for *DailyCandy* at *www.DailyCandy.com*, and use *Cash in the City* as a guidebook. Trust me, you can be an "It" girl and financially savvy at the same time. (You might even save some money for your progeny . . . ahem!)

September 4, 2001
Dany Levy
Founder, DailyCandy, Inc.

Acknowledgments

It is rare indeed when an author gets a gem of an idea like *Cash in the City*. Behind any successful great idea are a literary agent and book editor with the depth and vision to see the potential for such a book. For that, I thank Linda Konner and Debby Englander, executive editor at John Wiley & Sons, who continues to be a dream editor.

Also, thank you to Igor Bass, Annie Jennings PR; Terry Hines; Erica Pearson; Stacey Wilson; Wadene Howard; Rebecca Raphael; Rachel Elbaum; Donysha Smith; Pam Toussaint for accepting late-night panicked calls about the publishing business; Nick Chiles; Stephen Pollan; Bob Frare; Michael Bass; Trish McDermott at Match.com; Greg Friedman; Elke Villa; Joan O'Neil; Debra Manette; Michelle Mariano, Alexia Meyers, and Tess Woods at Wiley; Andy Stone at MacAllister Publishing Services; Walter Steinmann who owns Typhoon Brewery; Dad; Mom; Lillian Ayala; Doris Ellis; Chris Repetto whose staff painstakingly taught me how to work magic with Quicken; Sandy Kalman, Bob Casey, Janet Bamford, and Laura Lee at Bloomberg; Laura Hockridge, Sue Herrera, and Alex Crippen at CNBC; Mindy Reid and Tammy Warren in Los Angeles; Jeaneen Terio at Oppenheimer Funds; Dany Levy, Christina Nenov, and the hip, trendy Boston eatery Mantra; Bob Pickett; Jackie Blais; Rodney Brooks; Carrie Schwab Pomerantz; Bill W.; Mrs. Gaston; Mary Duffy at Kingworld; Laetitia and Clara Merzouk; Kelvin Boston; Elissa Rogovin; Alison Bamberger; and Jeff Penque.

CHAPTER 1

....

Introduction:
The Single,
Urban Woman Landscape

The single, urban, young woman needs *Cash in the City* as a guide-book to help her manage the money she makes and live a glam-orous lifestyle. Financial planners aren't interested in people who make less than $100,000 a year because they won't make much money off commissions from investing the client's money. As a result, the typical single, urban woman doesn't get professional financial advice because she will have a difficult time finding a plan-ner who will ever take her on as a client. Even if she does make $100,000 or more, most financial planners are not going to offer advice that's geared toward making the most of city living for a sin-gle woman. The planner won't have tips on how to decorate a sub-standard apartment or how to move ahead in a job or how to afford a chic cocktail dress for a pricey charity event.

Cash in the City includes basic financial advice in addition to offering tips on how to get into charity events for free and the pros vs. cons of living in a townhouse, co-op, condo, or single-family home.

The urban, single, young woman needs *Cash in the City* to avoid pitfalls that have put so many of her elders at a disadvantage. They include liquidating her retirement accounts instead of borrowing against them, spending a fortune on beauty rather than finding ways to look good for less, and settling for an average salary rather than negotiating a bigger one.

Single, urban women need their own financial planning book to help them navigate the big-city temptations that await them at every corner. They need to know how not to wind up like the old lady next door who never got out of her studio apartment and how to eat when unemployed.

In addition, *Cash in the City* can shed some light on city living for young single women thinking about moving to a big city and what they can expect. Women contemplating moving need their own financial planning book so that they can begin preparing for the big adjustment to city life. They need to know how to go about finding an affordable hair salon, an affordable-yet-attractive apartment, and the ins and outs of getting ahead on the job.

....

Example

Aline Romero moved to New York City from Biloxi, Mississippi, two years ago. The twenty-eight-year-old got a transfer from her job as a medical equipment sales representative. After a month in the Big Apple, the enormity of the challenge hit her.

"I never lived more than thirty minutes away from my family and friends. Isolation was the hardest feeling to overcome," she said.

The challenge was structuring a new life. Among the things Aline had to deal with were how to meet new friends, what parties to go to, and finding a place to get her stylish hair trimmed.

Aline makes double the money she made in Biloxi, but she also pays double the rent for her small studio apartment near noisy Times Square.

"If you're moving to the city, you're going to spend more on everything you do: food, manicures, cosmetics, wardrobe, and haircuts," she said, shift-

ing her weight from one flowered flip-flop to the other. "The good thing is there are more social things to do as a single person. The city is structured for people who are alone, who have no family or friends, and who are here to build a career."

Aline decided to do a summer share in the Hamptons. Knowing no one, she answered ads in the Village Voice for share houses in Southampton, East Hampton, and Bridgehampton. She also attended the annual Sand Bar at the Metropolitan Hotel, where many share houses gather to recruit members. Aline found a house she was comfortable with and made many new friends during her first summer in New York City.

....

Young, urban, single women tend to gravitate to glamour jobs, such as publishing, advertising, and entertainment, but those jobs don't earn them a lot of money. *Cash in the City* will guide readers on how to balance looking good for a job or a hot date on a measly paycheck, *Sex and the City*–style.

If you are a recent college graduate or young woman thinking about relocating to an urban center near you, these are things to consider:

- *Rent will be double in whatever city center you choose to move to.* Single women spent $4 trillion on housing, according to the Department of Labor's 1999 Consumer Expenditure Survey. Be prepared to step down a notch in your current living situation. You may be accustomed to modern appliances in your apartment. In the city, you may not have the luxury of space or you may have to make do with a tiny eat-in kitchen. In fact, your apartment building may be literally more than a hundred years old! Be prepared to adjust to a lower standard of living.

If you are too much of a princess to live in a beat-up studio, consider moving to the city with a buddy with whom you can share a renovated apartment. Although this may cramp your style, it may be the only way to afford an apartment in the center of the action of the city you choose. According to the U.S. Census Bureau, 3.7 million single women lived with roommates in the United States in 1998 compared to 18.7 million single women who lived alone. You may have more options if you're lucky enough to have parents who are willing to help you buy an apartment. In that case, Chapter 5 can give you pointers on buying a home in the city.

• *Expect food to be more expensive in city centers.* In suburban parts of the country, sprawling supermarkets sell bottles of water for 75 cents or less. In cities, expect smaller supermarkets with water going for at least $1.25 per bottle. Although 50 cents doesn't seem like much on the surface, it adds up over time.

Even though food is more expensive in urban grocery stores, it will be cheaper to eat at home in the city. Women spent $24.93 per week on food at home, according to the U.S. Department of Labor. Expect that amount to more than double once you move to the city because you won't be able to afford eating out as much as you did while living in Tyler, Texas. You may want to start watching the Food Channel to pick up tips on how to cook.

On the other hand, when living in the city, there will be many more opportunities to indulge in free food, especially if you take a glamour job in the entertainment or fashion business. There will be receptions and other events that offer shrimp appetizers. You can live off of that two or three times a week, but the rest of the week you're on your own.

Ramen noodles get old after a while, so practice cooking hamburgers, pasta, and fish.

Or if you're really bold and crafty, you can opt for cruising around the neighborhood like Beth Page. It may sound unbelievable, but some women have been known to do it.

• •

Example

When Beth Page moved to Boston from Jacksonville, Florida, she was unemployed. She had money to pay her rent but nothing left over to buy food. The twenty-five-year-old quickly befriended the restaurant owners and managers in her neighborhood.

"When I walked into a restaurant, they'd offer me wine. I would take bread instead and then they'd make me a salad," she said, twisting her silver ring on her pinky. "Or sometimes I'd ask the deli guy for a free sample. I'd go around to six or seven different delis for free samples and that would be dinner."

• •

- *Beauty will be more expensive in the city.* Single women spent nearly $6 trillion on personal care products and services in 1999, according to the Department of Labor. Whatever your budget for hair care, spa treatments, fitness, and perfume, increase it by at least 30 percent if you move to the city. Chapter 6 details ways around the high cost of beauty.

- *Clothing will be more expensive in the city.* Single women spent $187 trillion on apparel. If you're spending a modest amount now while living in Stillwater, Oklahoma, and you're planning on relocating to Atlanta, Georgia, you may want to continue to buy your clothes in Stillwater, where you can find fashionable clothes in upscale boutiques at a discount. There are also outlets on the outskirts of Atlanta where you can shop.

- *Parties and bars will be more expensive in the city.* If you're a recent college graduate, you may be used to happy hour specials at bars on campus, but the gravy train is over once you get into the real world of city living. While clubs in Bakersfield, California, may charge a $5 admittance fee, expect to pay triple that amount in Los Angeles or San Francisco.

Single women spent $14 trillion on entertainment and $27 trillion on alcohol in 1999. To reduce the amount you spend on partying, you may want to network among your college friends to get in on the house party circuit, where food and drinks are free and you won't have to pay an entry fee!

When you first move to the city, you'll need to create a new social circle.

....

Example

Sophie Janus found an upscale bar in Philadelphia and befriended the bartender. A Southerner, Sophie had no trouble striking up a conversation.

"When I moved to Philly, I knew no one. I went up to the bartender and asked him to make a good Sidecar," she said, adjusting her Chanel chain belt. "Then I asked him to tell me the ten places where I could find a good Sidecar and people who matched the way I was dressed."

The bartender took a napkin and wrote ten Philly hotspots with a black felt-tip pen.

"That's how I started. I just ventured off by myself and learned my way around the city," she said, pursing her lips. "I still have that list somewhere in my apartment."

Now, two years later, the media planner gets invited to free house parties every weekend.

....

Living in the city is different in that you may not need a car if you live in San Francisco, Boston, or New York. But even if you live in a city that requires driving, it will be different from living in the country. Another way that city living is different is that you may have to lock your doors when you leave your home. Often, in the country, people don't lock their front doors. But in the city, whether it's D.C. or Boston, the higher crime rate will require that you bolt your doors.

The single urban woman's life is different from the country-woman's life in ten critical ways:

1. The urban woman has to worry more about crime. That means she may need bars on her windows or a security system in her apartment. Living in a doorman building is safer but also costlier.

2. The urban woman deals with more traffic, which means that she'll be spending more time in her car or in a subway. Car insurance is also more expensive in urban centers.

3. The urban woman spends more on clothing. This means she will have to come up with economical ways to buy new clothes.

4. The urban woman spends more on food. She will have to learn to cook rather than eating out as much as she may be accustomed because eating in restaurants is more expensive.

5. The urban woman may have more exciting social opportunities, but, at the same time, those opportunities will be more expensive than in the country. For example, a charity benefit may cost $40 in Fayetteville, North Carolina, whereas in Raleigh-Durham a benefit could cost upward of $75.

6. The urban woman may have a more glamorous job than a countrywoman because jobs in entertainment, advertising,

and publishing are more likely to be located in big cities. But she'll have to look the part, which means spending more money on her appearance.

7. The urban woman may have a higher salary than someone living in the country, but that salary may not go as far in terms of buying groceries, paying for gym membership, or paying rent.

8. The urban woman may have access to more company benefits because she's more likely to work for a corporation than her sister who lives in Idaho.

9. The urban woman will feel more pressure to dress fashionably while living in the city whereas life in the country is more laid-back regarding clothing. Countrywomen won't be judged as harshly for wearing shorts and a T-shirt to work out; the city woman may feel the need to wear a matching outfit to the gym to fit in.

10. The countrywoman may feel more relaxed than her city counterpart because things are more stressful in the city. As a result, the single, urban woman may need more vacations.

This book contains advice that may be contrary to what some working women believe. Just as *Sex and the City* is over the top, some of the examples in *Cash in the City* seem outrageous too. But that doesn't mean that there aren't women out there like Samantha, Carrie, Miranda, and Charlotte who are just biding their time until Mr. Right strolls along. It may be old-fashioned, so if painting your nails, man-hunting, and highlighting your hair seems superficial and retro, pass GO and skip directly to the personal finance chapters that are filled with money strategies that can fill your pockets with cash so that you won't need a man.

Now that your fortunate situation in the big city has been explained, Chapter 2 details the money mistakes and pitfalls to side-step so that you are not compromised as Lily Bart's character was in Edith Wharton's classic, *The House of Mirth*.

Money Missteps to Avoid

Issues that Cloud the Single Woman's Financial Landscape

Today's single woman can be so blinded by the appeal of a certain lifestyle that she won't recognize a trap that can change her financial life forever. Imagine yourself skipping barefoot through a green forest with your long white summer dress whipping at your heels, a wreath of grape leaves crowning your head, and suddenly getting your foot stuck in a bear trap with no help in sight. Gone are your footloose and fancy-free days of dashing around oblivious to the dangers around you. You've been caught, and now you're paying the price.

Single women living in big cities tend to live for the moment because their money tends to be "me" money. In their twenties and thirties, they want to feel and look good with their money. It's about instant gratification and being entertained in all of your free time, which results in spending a lot of money. Given a choice of sitting home with a book or going out to a new movie, single women in urban settings are more likely to go where the action is.

There's nothing wrong with spending money on looking good and feeling good, but there is something wrong with spending all of your money—and not saving any for the future.

It's empowering for single women to have money all to themselves to do whatever they want to do. But this freedom can lead to a dead end later in life. Living in the moment has sound emotional advantages but also serious financial disadvantages.

This chapter will help you to avoid the many financial bear traps that abound in urban life.

Issue #1   *Women Earning Less than Men*

While women make up 46 percent of the workforce, they earned only about 76 cents for every dollar that men earned overall in 1999, according to the U.S. Department of Labor.

To make matters worse, a woman's earning power is limited by her occupation, and half of all women work in traditionally female, low-paying jobs without pensions, according to the Women's Institute for a Secure Retirement.

Three out of four working women earn less than $30,000 a year and nine out of ten earn less than $40,000 a year. Much of their income goes toward repaying debt, as women are more likely to be close to their credit limit.

One reason men make more than women is because women aren't as outspoken. It's imperative that single, urban women be their own advocates by speaking up for deserved promotions and by applying for traditionally male-dominated positions.

Women tend to be more deferential because they don't want to be perceived as pushy; they try to avoid the old adage that a woman who demands is considered aggressive while a man is considered ambitious.

One way to narrow the compensation gap and achieve more upward mobility is to get yourself noticed at work by speaking up and being more involved in decision making.

But according to a study, single women between the ages of twenty-one and thirty-four think more about family and relationships than they do about work and money. For example, when asked by Oppenheimer Funds which one of the following topics they think about most frequently, women responded this way:

Topic	Percentage
Work	13%
Sex	5%
Money	16%
Religion	6%
Family and relationships	57%
Sports	2%

When you're at work, instead of gabbing on the phone with girl-friends about boyfriend problems for an hour, cut the time you socialize on company time to thirty minutes and spend the remaining half hour researching an aspect of your position that interests you.

"The amount of money you make is directly related to how smart you work, and so what you want to do is to be sufficiently focused on work. That doesn't necessarily mean you have to work hard but that you make every minute count," says Barbara Raasch, a partner at Ernst and Young.

Issue #2 Believing the Rescue Fantasy That Marriage Will Save You

Another issue comes in the form of illusion for many single, urban women. They believe that Prince Charming will arrive and (as the old Calgon commercial says) "take me away." About 71 percent said they thought they'd get married in the future compared to only 24 percent who said no. A full 23 percent are delaying saving money for retirement because they think they will start saving *after* they are married!

This idea causes many women to not plan for their future and instead focus on attracting the man on the white horse by wearing the right shoes and perfume. There's nothing wrong with a good pair of Manolos and a glass bottle of Chanel No. 5, but whatever you have left over needs to be stashed away for the day when you can't wear spike heels.

Single women don't save because they continue to think that their future is going to change after they get married. It's almost as if they are waiting for their lives to begin, which can be dangerous because you may be single forever. You never know what this life has in store for you.

Start focusing on your financial future the day you start working by contributing to every investment vehicle—profit sharing and 401(k) plans—available to you through your company.

The trap is thinking: "My life is going to change. I don't have to save for retirement today. My husband will have money." Instead, look at life as if "this is it" and start providing for yourself in case Mr. Right turns out to be a no-show. Not every woman will be so lucky to marry old money like Charlotte did on *Sex and the City*.

The good news is that some women are saving, but instead of being in aggressive investments, they have their money in a savings bank. But, hey, some saving is better than none at all!

When asked by Oppenheimer Funds which of the following ways they are currently saving, women said:

Savings	Percentage
Through a 401(k) or 403(b)	27%
Company-provided pension plan	35%
Keogh, IRA, or SEP-IRA	15%
Savings account at a bank	66%
Brokerage or investment account	20%

Issue #3   Not Saving

About 48 percent of single young women live from paycheck to paycheck, according to an Oppenheimer Funds study. Fifty-four percent said they are more likely to acquire thirty pairs of shoes than have $30,000 in retirement assets. Some 33 percent said they would rather talk about their love life than talk to a financial advisor about investing.

These money details can be boring, but think of money as insurance in case your life doesn't work out as planned. Better to have more than enough than none at all.

The challenge is to stop spending and start saving.

What gets most women saving is that they earn more on the job. About 66 percent said they started earning enough money so they could put some aside for retirement. The second most cited reason was that their employer made it available.

Oppenheimer Funds asked women which events persuaded them to begin saving. Their responses:

Response	Percentage
I started earning enough money to set some aside	66%
My employer made it available	49%
Friends or family convinced me	46%
It just happened one day	45%
My employer matches contributions	42%
I read or heard in the media that it's important to invest	34%
I sat through a meeting at work and was convinced	19%
Had contact with a financial advisor	18%
I hit an age milestone	17%
I got married	8%

Issue #4   Greater Life Expectancy

Perhaps you'll be prompted to start stashing cash once the next statistic sinks in:

The life expectancy of women is much greater than men. Over 75 percent of women will live alone at some point in their life.

A longer life expectancy means that you will be living in retirement a lot longer than your mother did. Instead of dying at seventy-five, we'll be dying at ninety to one hundred years old and beyond, considering all of the medical advances being made today.

If you don't start saving, you could find yourself working at McDonald's when you're ninety years old, if the company is kind enough to hire you!

You're better off having ten pairs of shoes and $30,000 in the bank than thirty pairs of shoes and only $10,000 in the bank, because shoes wear out!

How to Avoid Becoming a Statistic

Prevent Debt

About 71 percent of women aged twenty-one to thirty-four wish they had greater control of their finances, but they don't do anything about it. For example, they allow the mountain of debt on credit cards to build. Debt is caused principally by the lack of focus on a budget. The best thing is to avoid credit cards altogether. Debt is like alcohol: If you have a problem with it, avoid it.

If you want a new TV, don't charge it. Wait until you've saved the money to buy it.

People tend to pay the minimum required payment amount on the credit card bill. Ideally, you want to pay off the balance each month.

Keep track of what you're charging throughout the month so that when a bill comes in the mail, you won't be flabbergasted. (See more on debt in Chapter 11.)

Increase Savings

To increase your savings rate, answer the following questions:

What are my current living expenses?
What do I need to spend?

The next step is to understand your short- and long-term goals. Make a list of your top five short-term goals and a list of your five long-term goals.

....

Example

Lucy Romanick is a thirty-two-year-old trading assistant at a financial firm in San Francisco. Her short-term goals are to vacation in Lake Tahoe, attend her best friend's wedding in Hawaii, buy a new couch for the living room, purchase a big Fendi purse, and get laser surgery to correct her vision. But when asked her long-term goals, Lucy was stumped. "Get married, I guess," she said sheepishly.

....

Getting married is not a financial goal! Appropriate financial long-term goals include financing your graduate degree, saving $1 million for retirement, earning $80,000 by the time you're forty-five years old, or buying a home.

Think up financial goals that will apply whether you get married or not and start stashing the cash necessary to reach those goals. For short-term goals of five years or less, use money market accounts. For long-term goals of ten years or more, invest in stock mutual funds.

How much you set aside in a savings account or investment vehicle on a monthly basis depends on your debt burden. But 10 percent of what you bring home is a good start.

"One of the best ways to store money is in a 401(k) plan if your company offers one. You can start by putting the maximum into that plan. Not only will you not pay taxes on it when it goes in, but it will be tax deductible on your tax returns," says Wendy Ehrlich, vice president of sales at Oppenheimer Funds.

Negotiating Your Way Up at Work

One way to avoid becoming one of those women who live paycheck to paycheck is to earn more money. You do that by moving up. To move up at work, you need to understand what your superiors think is important. Once you figure that out, you can structure your work so that you have those attributes.

It is very important to be connected appropriately. Determine who in your organization has power or is considered a rising star. Try to stay connected to them.

Finally, maintain a highly positive attitude. For example, don't criticize other people.

The positive way to get attention for your contributions is to mention them to someone who will tell the right people. The negative way to get attention for your contribution is to put down other colleagues—for example, "I produced ten reports this month and she only produced five."

Keep things positive!

Use the Internet

About 78 percent of Gen X women use the Internet, but not for investing purposes. This is a mistake. The Internet is a great way to learn more investment options and research investment performances.

You can learn a lot by surfing the Web. Try these websites for starters:

Yodlee.com

Morningstar.com

Quicken.com

TrowePrice.com

Even though young women are much more financially aware and motivated than their mothers were, they are still too reliant on the opinions of their family and friends. Women are much better off drawing their own conclusions based on expert advice and research.

When asked which of the following sources they rely on for advice, here are women's answers:

Advice Source	Percentage
Family and friends	43%
Stockbroker or financial planner	17%
Newspaper, magazines, or TV	11%
Employer	11%
Internet	8%
Coworkers	5%

Ten Money Mistakes Single Urban Women Should Avoid

1. Living paycheck to paycheck
2. Spending all of your cash on hand
3. Carrying over a debt balance at the end of the month
4. Procrastinating about retirement
5. Expecting Prince Charming to change your life
6. Not keeping track of your spending
7. Not investing in your 401(k) at work
8. Laziness on the job
9. Relying on parents, friends, or boyfriends to make your financial decisions
10. Not seeking professional help from a fee-only financial planner or financial advisor

The next chapter will teach you how to buy a Prada bag and have money left over to save for when you're not so cute in that miniskirt. In other words, you're going to learn how to streeeeeettttcccccchhhhh your dollars without snapping at the seams!

CHAPTER 3

....

Stretching Your Dollars

In the city, single women are likely to be so busy with achieving-success classes at the Learning Annex and sipping Bellinis at trendy bars that they throw away handfuls of money without realizing it. One way to get a handle on your spending is to keep track of everything that goes out. File away receipts in your wallet in order to keep track of your expenditures when you get home later in the evening. Do this for at least a month. The more numbers you have, the more accurate your spending plan will be. Ideally, three months of expenses can give you a picture of your spending habits.

Sample Daily Spending Log
August 2, 2001

	Expense	Category
Magazine	$3.99	Leisure
Manicure	$8.00	Grooming
Tip	$1.00	Gratuity
Lip & Eye Waxing	$25.00	Grooming
Dinner at deli	$6.61	Food
Chanel jacket/resale shop	$70.00	Clothing

Once you've gathered numbers, categorize each expenditure and tally up how much you spent for the week on food, clothes, utilities, books, music, nightclubs, and so on. Once you have four weeks of numbers, you can log them in for the thirty days. If you're spending $500 a month on nightclubs, you can aim to cut that in half.

Or if you're spending $400 on taxis, a future goal can be to reduce the amount by $150.

The idea is to rein in your spending where you are excessive and spend more where you are negligent. For example, are you spending enough on self-care, such as massages and dentist appointments? You may want to beef up the self-care categories by $100 if you're only spending $50 a month in those areas.

After you've created your spending plan, you still have to keep track of your daily expenditures to make sure that you are not going over or under your allotted amounts. (See Chapter 12 for an easy way to do this.)

It may sound tedious, but it will help you to have more money left over each month. Vagueness about money leads to not having enough money and ultimately more debt, because if we don't have the cash, most of us put it on a credit card.

··

Example

Christina Voutsinas says living in New York City draws her out to meet people and to be in the scene. But being in the scene requires a certain image.

The account coordinator estimates that a third of her salary goes to the latest fashions. That's about $10,000 to $15,000 a year, or about $500 a month. Another third of her salary goes to bills. She spends about $40 to $45 a month on manicures and eyebrow and lip waxing. The rest goes to eating out.

The cappuccino-lover pays $750 for an apartment in Manhattan's trendy Chelsea. If she carries a credit card balance, it's no more than $300, and she pays it off in two months.

"If I buy something on my credit card, I try to be more conscious for like a month or two by cutting back on eating or drinking out because drinks in Manhattan cost an average of $12. I also cut back on taxis and take the subway instead," she said. "A little debt, like $300 on a credit card, is fine with me. But I would never put myself in the $1,000 range."

The twenty-four-year-old holds it all together on her $30,000 a year salary with the help of her mother and father.

"My parents contribute about $7,000 a year to help me live a nice lifestyle. They're really supportive of me being able to go places and travel," she says. *"Mom is very helpful. Usually if I go shopping with her, she'll buy my basics or my makeup. I don't think I'd be able to have the things that I have without them."*

The self-professed shoe addict says without their help, she'd be working three jobs to maintain her lifestyle. "I already bought ten pairs of shoes this season. That's what makes me happy!"

If Christina kept track of her expenses on a daily basis, she probably wouldn't have to use credit cards at all because she'd spend less money, knowing where her cash goes.

....

Envelope Technique

Saving money doesn't have to mean going to the bank and depositing money into a savings account. It can be as simple as setting aside an envelope on your dresser or underneath your pillow. In this envelope, you put whatever extra cash you have left over at the end of the day. Whether it's $2 or $10 left over from a night on the town with your fashion designer friend, it starts to add up. You'll be surprise how fast you can accumulate $100 in a few weeks from stashing extra dollars in this way.

Set aside envelopes for each short-term goal you have in mind. For example, you may have an envelope to save for a weekend getaway, an envelope for a Fendi purse you've been eyeing, and an envelope for a facial at a pricey spa.

If you really want to get creative, decorate the envelopes with pictures of your goal.

Creative Ways to Save Money

Just as we watch what we eat, some of us have no choice but to watch what we spend. This list will give you ideas on how to stretch your dollars in the big city.

Food

- Eat at hip trendy restaurants for lunch rather than dinner in order to save on food bills.

- Buy a Brita water filter to drink water from the faucet rather than buying bottled water. Fill up empty water bottles with filtered water to take to work for the week.

Leisure

- Borrow books, audiotapes, CDs, and videos from the library.

- Trade books, CDs, and videos with reliable girlfriends whom you know will return them.

- Join the local Y instead of an expensive gym.

- Buy a bike instead of joining a gym, or jog in your local park.

- Attend free arts and entertainment events in your city.

- Volunteer for your local opera house or theater in order to see shows for free.

- Join biking, swimming, or running clubs. Not only is it cheaper than a gym, it's a great way to meet men!

- Quit smoking, drinking alcohol, and drinking coffee. These are expensive habits that add up over time. Besides, cigarettes stain your teeth, alcohol ages you faster, and caffeine makes some people nervous!

Travel

- Vacation close to home, a place you can get to by car or train in just a few hours.

- Sign up with the Appalachian or Adirondack Mountain Club (*www.outdoors.org*) or Sierra Club. These organizations offer group hiking trips near lakes for as low as $25 per weekend (including lodging, food, and transportation).

- Use your credit card company's insurance coverage when renting a car to avoid paying for duplicate insurance coverage from the rental company.

- Book airline travel at least twenty-one days in advance or comparison shop to find the best prices. Check out the individual airline websites and *www.orbitz.com* and *www.lastminutetravel.com*.

- Order plane tickets from *www.Cheaptickets.com*.

Transportation

- Switch from premium to regular gasoline if your car allows it.

- Keep your tires inflated to the right level. It gets you better mileage.

- Change the air filter in your car yourself. Get a cute mechanic to show you how!

- Carpool with favorite coworkers. In some cities, you can speed through traffic faster at rush hour by taking advantage of the special "high-occupancy vehicle" (HOV) lanes and save on gas.

...phone and Internet

- Use phone cards that you buy from the drugstore to make your long-distance phone calls. It ensures that you only talk for the amount of time you purchased.

- Switch to a free Internet service provider, such as *www.net-zero.com*.

- Get free long-distance phone service over the Internet. Try *www.bigredwire.com, www.dialfreecalls.com, www.freeway.com, www.hotvoice.com, www.phonebridge.com*, or *www.smartprice.com*.

- Whenever you get a lower-rate offer from a long-distance phone company, call your existing phone company to see if it will beat it.

- Buy your cell phone secondhand, refurbished.

- Buy insurance for your cell phone so that if you lose it, you only have to pay a nominal replacement fee.

- Find phone numbers on the Internet at *www.555-1212.com* instead of dialing 411.

- Look for free samples on the Internet, such as Oil of Olay at *www.coolfreebielinks.com, www.e-goodz.com, www.freebieclub.com, www.freesamples.com, www.startsampling.com*, and *www.total-effect.com/sample/sample.shtml*.

Shopping

- Buy cosmetics from the drugstore instead of the department store. You can save hundreds of dollars.

- Become a mystery shopper. Visit *www.mysteryshop.org, www.secretshopnet.com*, and *www.mysteryshopperjobs.com*.

- If you live in the New York area, shop at Woodbury Commons Premium Outlet, which includes Chanel, Fendi, and Christian Dior merchandise for up to 75 percent off. Similar outlets in other parts of the country include the Sawgrass Outlet in South Florida, the Tanger Outlet Center at Locust Grove in Atlanta, Georgia, and the Saks and Ann Taylor outlets at the Great Mall of Milpitas near San Jose, California.

- Barter! For example, offer to do public relations for a small boutique in exchange for gift certificates or a discount on clothing.

- Avoid buying clothes that are "dry clean only."

- Buy gifts off season and when they are on sale.

- Get a second job at your favorite clothing store. That way, you make money and get a discount on outfits!

- Buy a facial steamer to do your own facials rather than going to the salon.

- Wax your own eyebrows and lips, if you dare!

Financially

- Looking for a quick, easy, and legal way to make cash? Participate in focus groups. Market research companies pay participants for their time. One company that conducts focus groups is the Murray Hill Center. They have offices in New York City (212-685-0571), Chicago (312-803-445), Los Angeles (310-392-7337), and Atlanta (404-495-1434). Visit *www.murrayhillcenter.com* for more information. Or visit *www.focusvision.com* for market research companies around the country.

- Authorize an automatic transfer of $100 a month out of checking into a savings account.

- Don't use overdraft protection for your checking account. A daily interest rate accrues if you don't pay the overdraft right away.

- Make ATM withdrawals only from your home bank. You save $1.50 for not using an out-of-network bank.

- Bank with a savings bank or credit union rather than a commercial bank to save on fees.

- Transfer your balance to a low-interest credit card and use one that has no annual fee. Visit *www.creditdawg.com* to find appropriate credit cards.

- Join a professional organization to get a discount on health insurance if you are self-employed.

Home

- Buy furniture from retirees who have recently downsized and are looking to get rid of stuff. Look for home sales in the newspaper or ask Mom and Dad about family friends.

- Compare the energy efficiency rating on any new appliances you buy.

Once you get the hang of stretching your dollars, you may find yourself wondering what to do with all of the extra cash. How about sprucing up the crash pad? Chapter 4 explains how to do it on a budget.

CHAPTER 4

....

Your Home or Your Heels

Importance of a Quality Home

Single women living in cities tend to live in smaller places because rent is more expensive in urban areas. This makes their home less likely to be the center of their social life. The city tends to be their living room.

Women living in country environments are more likely to spend money at Home Depot to beautify their homes because they may not have as active a social life as women living in big cities, and they may have bigger and better homes. Urban, single women in their twenties and thirties tend to skimp on their apartments so that they can afford to look more glamorous. That approach might be okay for the first few years out of college, but eventually you'll want a better place to live because one day Mr. Right will want to see your home.

Like it or not, most men like to see that a woman has some ability to create a pleasing environment. Even though the women's movement liberated us from lots of boring stuff, such as staying at home and doing the laundry, the fact remains that it's still the woman who provides the food and a comfortable, decorated home.

The energy you feel when you wake up in your apartment sets the mood for the day, the week, the month, the year, and your life. It won't matter how much money you have to spend on clothes, your hair, shoes, or makeup if you're living in a box. How you feel about yourself is more important than the way that other people perceive you.

We, as complex human beings, are affected by our surroundings. So, if you live in a shack, you may not have as much self-esteem when you face the world.

"When you live in a dump and you get ready in the morning in a dump, there will be a part of you that is still connected to what's not working in your life, which could affect other areas of your life," says Marilyn Graman, founder of Life Works, an organization that helps women understand how men think.

"The same thing happens with a date. Thinking 'If he only saw what I just walked out of he'd never like me' can linger in the back of your mind and affect the way you feel about yourself."

Affording a Home

So, how can you get out of a dump and into a nicer apartment?

For one thing, you can make more money. (See Chapter 7.)

Or you can get a roommate in order to afford a bigger and better place. Alternatively, you can move to the outskirts of the city, where rent is often cheaper.

All of these options have advantages and disadvantages. If you don't want to leave a trendy address within the city limits, you can fix up the dump you live in, which takes some investment of time, labor, and money.

Save money by taking the time to figure out what you want. Price shopping and getting friends to help can cut down on expenses.

Organize a party around renovating and decorating your abode. Lay out some chips and dip, pop the cork on a bottle of Moët & Chandon, and invite your friends over to make it fun. Oh, and don't forget your favorite music!

∙∙

Example

When Emily Donahue moved to Boston from upstate New York after graduating from college in 1997, she rented a $500 apartment in a beach town in the suburbs. Not many people wanted to live there because it was close to the airport and noisy.

"It's a nice community but like a little dry town. There is not a whole lot going on there. So it wasn't quite what I was looking for, but I couldn't afford anything else expensive because you can't really move in anywhere without laying out four months' rent," Emily said.

Even though her rent was affordable, she was spending a lot of money on incidentals, such as cab rides because she lived so far away from the city.

"I really did try and cook my own food and certainly not hang out in very swank areas, but just going out in general turned into $100 a night because it involved drinks, food, catching a flick, and then a ride home in a cab," she said. After two years, the media specialist realized that sharing and living closer to the city would be more cost effective in the long run because she would save on cab fare.

Today, the twenty-six-year-old shares a three-bedroom with two other women, pays $600 for an $1,800 apartment, and lives a block away from the Brookline subway station.

"It's convenient and I don't have to worry about getting a car. Owning a car in Boston is almost more expensive than living when it comes to parking," she said. Emily's new apartment is spacious and visitors are impressed with its splendor. "I've seen people who are living in great areas of the city but their studios look like tiny closets. So when people come over to our huge place, it's a big deal," she said.

She found her apartment through www.apartments.com. "I answered ads of people who had rooms in their apartments around the city. I interviewed with a bunch of people in about ten or twelve different apartments and then found my roommates, who were great. Once I did that, I was spending less money per month on rent and saved on cabs because I was in the city," she said.

One of the cons of her new apartment is having roommates, but Emily feels she has no choice. "The fact is, if I want to stay living in the city, I won't be able to do it on my own with the debt that I have because one of my goals is to clear up those credit cards and pay my student loans back," she said.

....

Tips for Selecting a Roommate

1. Make sure your potential roommate has the same lifestyle.

2. Look for someone who has some flexibility.

3. Someone who has experience sharing will be easier to get along with.

4. Pick someone who views neatness in the same way you do.

5. Discuss how you will share expenses before you move in to determine your attitudes about money.

Finding Your Urban Home

Most people find their first urban apartment through the classifieds or word of mouth. Sometimes the best deals come about through the grapevine. That means you have to talk about what you're looking for to anybody and everybody who will listen.

Alternative means include roommate services and brokers.

But first you have to know what you're looking for. Write up a list of your apartment criteria. Do you want an elevator, a doorman, or a particular neighborhood? These are all features to think about before looking.

Once you decide what you want, it's time to pound the pavement. If you look long enough, you'll find what you want.

Be willing to compromise on some of the things on your list. If you have twelve items on your list and you find an apartment that fits ten, you may want to jump on it.

Once you find an affordable apartment that you like, do everything that you can to hold on to it.

....

Example

Elizabeth Setedl pays $650 a month for an apartment in Los Angeles. The twenty-seven-year-old sends cards and cookies to the landlord every month to keep on good terms.

"They called me once to raise the rent. I started crying that I'm a good citizen, that they shouldn't do it. So they didn't," she said, her corkscrew brown curls obscuring her hazel eyes. "Anyway, it's true. I am a good citizen."

Elizabeth also treats her neighbors kindly, which has paid off at least once. When she went on a business trip, she asked the people who hung out on the corner to look out for her car, which was a brand-new Honda Accord. "When I came back, my car had been washed twice," she said, breaking into a gap-toothed grin.

....

Apartment Essentials

Once you find your apartment, there are some bare necessities that you will need to conform to societal expectations.

You'll need airy, throw pillows for the couch, a coffee table, a kitchen table, cooking ware, an armoire, a stereo, a television, a sofa that seats at least two people, a comfortable bed, curtains or blinds, and a down comforter.

Throw in some candles, fresh flowers, a couple of pictures or paintings on the wall, mirrors, colorful light, and magazines.

"The fresh flowers don't have to be expensive. They can be daisies or carnations. Candles always add romance. Pictures on the wall don't have to be expensive. They can be movie posters that are free, but they have to mean something to you," says Suzanne Goldberg, president of SBG Design, an interior-decorating firm. "A mirror in the entryway opens up the room. Don't just put a roll-up shade on your windows. A valance that goes across the top of your windows in simple fabric or simple design adds softness."

Entertaining Men in Your Home

Some teary-eyed woman may be reading this chapter after a man has dumped her because her apartment is below standard. Of course, he'll never tell you that. But if a man does dump you because of your apartment, be glad he left. If he's really into you, he'll help you fix up your apartment the way that Aidan refinished Carrie's floors when they first started dating.

"It says something about him, that he's not flexible enough to include your style or that this living thing is very important to him. If it's not very important to you, then it would be something you would fight over," says Marilyn Graman.

If you're decorating to please, use the color blue in your apartment because men like blue. But don't flood the apartment with lots of flowers or frills because it makes them uncomfortable. Mix frills with solids and stripes.

Make sure your sheets aren't too girly. Men don't like sleeping in women's sheets. Next time you're in a department store, compare the women's sheets with the men's sheets. There really is a difference!

When a man is at your pad, use candles to provide mood, and make sure you have lamps that dim so he can kiss you romantically.

A neat apartment scores lots of points, but you don't want to seem so neat that you appear compulsive. "He wants to be able to put his feet up. He wants to be able to eat while sitting on the sofa. And you don't want too much clutter," Graman said.

If you want him to stay or come back, make room for him to put his keys down. Create space in your closet so that subconsciously he will know that there is a place for him to hang his suit or play clothes for the next day.

Things That Turn Men Off About Women's Apartments

- Too many flowers
- Decorated all in black
- Photo of an ex-boyfriend
- No coffee table for his feet
- Too messy
- Too neat
- Clutter
- No stereo system
- Too frilly
- Empty fridge
- Dumpy bed
- Too many pets
- No VCR system

Decorating Your First Urban Apartment

If you don't have much money to buy nice furniture, you can get away with buying cheap furniture and covering it with some interesting fabric. For example, you can buy a round wooden table with stick legs for about $10 to $15 and throw a cool tablecloth over it.

Your coffee table can be orange crates with a board on it, but if you cover it with fabric from old clothes, it can be chic or creative.

You'll want to have a nice matching set of forks and knives that serve four people.

Colors in your apartment should be those that you like, but also put in some neutral colors that blend. For example, if you really like purple, you may want to throw on off-white, black, or navy to offset it.

You could have a solid-colored purple sofa with patterned pillows that add a snap to your environment. Pillows on your sofa are an inexpensive accessory that add warmth and more dimension to the room. "For sofas, it may be cheaper if you're less choosy and go for styles that are more common because that's what you'll find left over at sales and that's what you'll find marked down lower to begin with," says Kimberlee Hanson, an interior designer and owner of Chipped Cup in Highland Park, New Jersey.

Although outfitting your house in solids is probably safer, it can be boring. Instead, mix floral with solid or a texture pattern with a smaller floral pattern. If you don't want too much floral, substitute it with more geometric patterns. As long as all the colors coordinate, you should be okay.

"Lighter colors are softer and soothing and you don't get sick of them as quickly, but if you like brighter colors add them in smaller pieces and in your accessories," says Goldberg.

∙∙

Example

Rosie O'Neill lives and works in Los Angeles as an account executive. The twenty-two-year-old pays $750 for a studio apartment in West Hollywood. When she invited friends over, she felt embarrassed because her apartment was very dark and had no life.

"I've always been the type of person who wears bright-colored clothes and I have a light, bright personality, but my apartment didn't match my personality at all and I was ashamed to have people come over," she said.

The first thing she did was paint the walls light green to lighten up the apartment. Then she went to a warehouse where film studios sell their discarded props from movies and bought about $400 worth of decorations.

"I bought some things that are unusual but that look kind of cute. I bought a little picket fence and filled it with silk flowers, some oversized ladybugs, and mushrooms. It's kind of like a fun fairy-tale garden," Rosie said. "Plants are what make my apartment look bigger than it is. I have plants and flower pots in there." She bought a red velvet couch from Ikea for $1,100, and her parents gave her a bed. Her boyfriend at the time helped her paint and put up wall cabinets. Prior to decorating, Rosie had one glaring, bright light in the middle of the room.

"I bought a few of those halogen lamps that are on stands. Now everything is lit from the ground up so it looks a lot warmer. I added Christmas lights to decorate the picket fence and the garden, which looks really pretty," she said. "I also have some spotlights that I hide in different places."

The only drawback is that her apartment can get messy with all of its accessories. She cleans the apartment once a week and cleans the props thoroughly once a month.

"It's worth it. Now that I've decorated, it's fun to have people over. It's my way to show off that I've made a tiny space look unique, bright and fun," she said.

∙∙

Decorating on a Budget

Start your decorating kick by getting an idea of what you want. Look through decorating trade magazines or leaf through decorating books at the bookstore in order to get a sense of style.

To afford decorating your apartment, start saving a fixed amount of money each week. If it's $20 a week, after three weeks, you'd have enough to buy two or three throw pillows, two nice candles, a matching set of dishes, and pretty fabric that you can toss over your ugly or used sofa.

Word of mouth works for furniture too. Let everyone know that you're collecting furniture. People who are getting married or friends of the family who are downsizing would love the opportunity to unload some furniture.

Spend your Saturday afternoons visiting thrift stores and flea markets.

If you don't have money for artwork and you have an artistic flair, frame and hang your own artwork on the walls. If you can't draw or paint, make a collage using pictures from magazines or photos from your childhood.

If buying new furniture isn't in your budget, restore your existing furniture with new fabric or new finish.

Listen and read for the annual, quarterly, and monthly sales at Pottery Barn, Crate and Barrel, and department stores in your city.

You also could put an ad in the local paper saying that you are a young single woman looking for nice furniture with which to furnish your apartment. There are rich people in the city who will give their furniture to a worthy soul rather than putting it on the street.

Psychology of Lights

If you want to make a big difference fast because you have a hot date on Saturday, use lights.

Having the right lights can light up your life and your spirit because light has a psychological effect on mood.

Use track lighting with smaller heads, standing halogens, task lights, table lamps, and three-way lamps.

Accentuating with Lights

Create the illusion of space with a floor lamp that points up at the ceiling. Add dimmers so that you can change the mood by lowering the light with the flip of a switch.

In addition to lighting the ceiling to make a room look larger, you can light the walls. If you do that evenly, it pushes the wall out.

"A lot of times you have some kind of light right in the middle of the room. You can replace it with light that has a diffused look to it so that it throws light not just down but out to the sides. That helps the room looks larger. If the light is only aimed down, then it tends to make the room look smaller," says Pamela Horner, manager of Lighting Education at Osram Sylvania, a lighting manufacturer in Danvers, Massachusetts.

In the kitchen, create the illusion of space by adding a light underneath the cabinets. They're simple to install. Some even plug in so that you can take them with you when you move. A cabinet light illuminates nooks and crannies. Plus it's a lot easier to cut up your vegetables when you're cooking. But make sure you clean the cracks before bringing attention to those nooks and crannies.

The worst thing is having a 500-watt bulb in the middle of your apartment with no shade on it. It produces a maddening glare.

Highlight or bring attention to a painting or favorite poster by putting light on it. Aim a halogen light at it or plug in track lighting underneath it.

Be careful what color you use to highlight paintings or other objects. If you're trying to illuminate something green and you put a red light on it, you're not going to get the results you want. Instead, use soft pastel colors.

For a simple change, use colored light bulbs, such as pink, amber, and soft blue. Pink bulbs in your bedside or bureau lamp beautify the apartment by giving it a glowing look, and it's flattering to all skin tones. Make sure the colored bulbs match the lampshade's color too.

With fluorescent strip lighting, you can add colored gel (from the theater shops) to cover the light. "It's a very cool light source to the touch. It's not going to burn anything up. You could put it on a shelf, which gives a nice colored wash where you want it. Then you can change it for Christmas or Easter or whatever," says Horner. You can put simple colored glass filters over track lights or floor-mounted lights that take a reflector lamp.

Lighting also can be used to conceal a bad paint job, cracked walls, peeling paint, or uneven walls. To take attention away from the walls, light something else near it. For example, highlight a picture on the wall with a narrow beam of light. Guests won't notice the wall because their attention will be on the picture.

If there are irregularities on your wall, don't graze the wall with light; doing so will maximize the imperfections. But if you have exposed brick in your apartment, then you would want to graze the wall with light to bring out the texture.

Cost of Lighting

Incandescent lights cost the least. Second are halogens, which are energy efficient. They help to cut down the electric bill. Third in the hierarchy are fluorescent lights.

"If, however, you take the long-term view of two or three years, the list reverses itself," says Horner. "That's because you have to count the money you're spending to keep the lights on and the money you're paying in utilities. In the long run, the lowest cost is fluorescent."

The bare minimum that you need is a decorative lighting fixture for your main living area, such as a chandelier or an antique lamp. With that, you're not only decorating with light but you're decorating with a fixture. You can find nice affordable antiques with old silk shades and fringe and chandeliers at flea markets.

Another essential item is a functional task light, which is portable and can be floor mounted or put on a tabletop. You want one that is articulated, which means you can move the head and the arm, adjusting the placement of light. Aim the light at the book you're reading or aim it up at the ceiling to open up the room.

Curtains

If you have curtains, you can get away without having blinds if you're far enough away from other buildings and there's no clear view. A thick curtain in a dark color can eliminate the need for blinds. But a sheer curtain that allows sunlight to come through the window may require blinds. Ikea is a great place to go for affordable blinds and curtains.

"You can get the matchstick blinds or a lot of different wooden blinds for very little money in different colors. They have about three or four different shades, including pine and walnut," says Hanson.

White, sheer curtain panels cost $5 to $7. Pottery Barn also has relatively inexpensive curtain panels.

If you're crafty with your hands, you can sew them yourself because the bulk of fabric is about the right width for any standard curtain. Just add a loop at the top and a seam.

If you have a valance, you can add a blind underneath it. The valance adds fabric to the room without getting too expensive.

Although your curtains don't have to match your comforter, make sure all of the colors coordinate.

Loft Beds

If putting your bed on stilts allows you to have more living space, it could be a good idea. But be mindful that you'll be climbing up a ladder every night in order to crawl into bed. It can be cozy and romantic, but it also can get old very quickly. Loft beds have their place when you're in college and maybe your first apartment, but there are safety concerns in the long run. People have been known to fall out of their loft beds. If a loft bed is already in the apartment when you move in, you may as well use it, but if you build one from scratch, it may take some getting used to.

Ten Home Decorating Secrets

1. Have an idea of what you want before starting.

2. Trust your instincts when you're shopping. Don't second guess yourself if something appeals to you.

3. Always measure things before buying them. Bring a tape measure when you're shopping.

4. Decide on your favorite colors.

5. Use candles, draped fabric, artwork, mirrors, and flowers to accentuate your environment.

6. Leave room in your budget for great finds.

7. Don't buy everything at once. Furnishing your home should be a long-term project.

8. Hunt around on the streets of wealthy neighborhoods, and don't be ashamed to take home a nice piece of furniture.

9. Don't start jamming any piece of furniture in your apartment to fill it up. Less is more.

10. Spread the word among family and friends that you're willing to accept free, used furniture.

After you've decorated your apartment and lived in it a few years, there may come a time when you realize you're throwing money away on rent. It may dawn on you that you could use the tax deduction of owning your own home. In that case, Chapter 5 gives you the lowdown on buying your first home.

CHAPTER 5

···

Buying a Home

Issues for Young Single Women

If you're not being whisked away by a wealthy doctor like Charlotte on *Sex and the City*, you may want to consider buying a home for yourself. That doesn't mean a house with a white picket fence and SUV in the driveway. It could mean buying your apartment when the building goes co-op.

When buying a home, young single women living in the big city face a greater challenge than their married counterparts. First, the mortgage applicant has only one income. As a result, it is often harder to qualify for a mortgage. It can also be a challenge to make financial decisions without having someone to bounce ideas off of.

Single, urban women look for different amenities in a home than married couples. Safety is usually number one, along with convenience, such as being able to run errands nearby. A couple or a family might be willing to drive a little farther to get groceries whereas a single woman might want a more intimate community where everything is within walking distance.

Why Buy?

Renting is as good as throwing money away while buying is an investment and tax writeoff. Generally, for the first five or six years of a loan, 96 to 98 percent of your payments go for interest. So if your mortgage is $2,000 a month, multiply that by 98 or 96 percent, which gives you $1,920 a month. Over the course of twelve months, you will accrue $23,000 in tax write-offs.

Along with working and having your own money, having a home adds another layer of assets that appreciate over time. For single women specifically, says Valentina Barbatelli, a senior manager for Coldwell Banker in Milwaukee, buying a home solidifies the notion that you are in charge of your own destiny. And it feels good to be an owner. The satisfaction of having their own home is a big reason single women buy.

Pros and Cons of Buying in the City

Most people see the urban home purchase as the ultimate Catch-22. On one hand, you have great potential for price inflation to resell because the turnover is quicker, and there is a constant influx of people buying and selling. Chaz Walters, a Chicago-based broker with Coldwell Banker, says that city living also affords you the convenience of having things at your disposal. "You have everything within a couple of feet or a couple blocks," says Walters.

Some would say the opportunities of urban living are not only great but boundless in large cities, especially for an unmarried woman. Culture, the arts, shopping, sporting events, business prospects: It's all a short ride away. Having no yard or lawn to maintain is also very attractive to the avid woman traveler and weekend warrior.

Despite high rent in big cities, buying a home can be easier because incomes are generally—but not always—commensurate with the cost of living. "Yes, it's more expensive to live here, but the income is so much better in a big city than in a small city. I think the small cities pay according to their lifestyle," says Lela Leong, a home loan manager for Countrywide Home Loans in Los Angeles.

But in the end, this "great" life has its price, as most single wo-men's salaries do not and cannot stretch as far as they would in rural areas. The downside is that city living leaves people little elbow room. Dense overpopulation is the unavoidable trade-off of living in metropolitan areas that never sleep.

For women with stable careers, buying a home is probably one of the smartest things they can do because of the tax benefits that go along with making a monthly investment that increases in value. Many homes will give their owners excellent returns.

"I don't know where you can get $100,000 back in five years," says Leong. "There is no other way that you can make that kind of return. You can be lucky in the stock market, but the stock mar-ket is not going to provide you housing. Real estate is a solid invest-ment, always has been."

Buying with a Friend

So, maybe you can't afford to buy a home on your own, and you're still dateless on Saturday night. This may be a perfect time to buy a home in partnership with a friend. It's a big trend in urban areas for single women to buy homes together.

Before you consider buying with a friend, sit down and work through what kind of lifestyle you want, your expectations, and consult with a real estate agent and attorney to evaluate options for taking a title in partnership with someone who is not your spouse or lover.

When entering into such a partnership, you must put all verbal agreements in writing because being single is not always a perma-nent situation. What happens if one of you loses her job and can't pay the mortgage? What happens if one of you has a boyfriend who stays for weeks at a time? Or if one of you marries? Before buy-ing in partnership, talk about all the different scenarios that could present themselves.

....

Example: Evelyn Michelle Darden

For some women, still being single in their thirties is a point of concern and worry for their financial and reproductive futures. For others, such as Evelyn Darden, a D.C.-based consultant, being a single, thirty-something professional was the perfect time to make the ultimate commitment.

After living in a two-bedroom, Dupont Circle condo for nearly eight years, Evelyn felt she needed more space and some distance from the city and her increasingly crowded neighborhood. She decided she wanted to buy a brownstone, but with the market at its unforgiving price levels, she knew she couldn't do it alone. So she hit the Rolodex. "I decided to partner with a friend of mine with whom I had worked in the past," says Evelyn. "Neither one of us was in a serious relationship at the time."

With the help of a real estate agent, Evelyn found a five-bedroom home on Canyon Street in Columbia Heights, Maryland. She's lived there now for eighteen months.

Evelyn and her cobuyer were lucky to find a lender who was supportive of what they were trying to do. He took the time to get to know them as clients and understand their partnership. "He recognized that not many people were trying to do what we were doing," she says.

Getting used to a mortgage wasn't a big adjustment. "In the end, you are still paying rent. You've got to pay your rent or you won't have a place to live. It's the same way with a mortgage." The irony is that Evelyn was paying more in rent than her current monthly home mortgage.

Pairing up with another single person had plenty of perks. Splitting the bills, fixing problems, maintaining a yard, and overall logistics of living were made simple. And the financial rewards were almost instant. "We bought our house for $185,000 and we closed in March of 2000," Evelyn says. "Ten months later, not even a year, we got an offer for $285,000 on the home, and we just appraised it at $315,000 about three months ago."

Their exit strategy is to move out, rent the home, and split the rental income. If the women choose to sell, they'll split the profits. But the neigh-

borhood is doing so well that Evelyn doesn't think they'll be selling any-time soon.

The thirty-five-year-old isn't alone in her decision to partner up. The Washington Post ran a story on the trend of young single women in D.C. buying homes with friends. "I think our society is not really structured for the new lifestyle that we have now," she said.

....

Housing Options

Once you've committed to taking the plunge into homeownership, what do you buy?

For single women, there are many options for urban ownership, including condos, co-ops, townhouses, and single-family homes. Being single, you will probably want to be in a community that has a lot of other singles. The condominium community might be your best option, because the units are smaller and there is little exterior maintenance.

However, if you are a dedicated green thumb or animal lover, you might want to look at a single-family house that has a front and backyard.

Evaluate your circumstances. Do you need a large yard for your St. Bernard? Is it close to your work? For many, having a short commute to work is as good as gold. Is recreation important to you? For example, if you are a cyclist, is it important to have bike paths nearby? Do you want to live in a neighborhood that has tennis courts? What role, if any, will your spiritual life play in where you choose to live? For many, having churches and synagogues nearby is a major factor in quality of life. And if you have health concerns, are you near a hospital or doctor? All of these factors should play into your decision, or else you'll be sorry later when you find yourself in a remote part of town.

Whatever you buy, make sure it's something that could easily be sold again, and that chances are good you'll see a profit from when you sell in the future.

Condos

In opting for a condo, look for one that has low assessments or, rather, one that appreciates at a much quicker rate. Typically, low-assessment condos do not offer services such as doormen, valet, indoor garage parking, and the like.

Condos especially are rife with "hidden assessments," such as payments you might have to make for new windows or a new roof. When you review the condo contracts, look very carefully for pending assessments. For this type of information, scour the minutes of a condo association meeting report.

Co-op versus Condo

The biggest difference in qualifying for buying a condo versus a co-op is that co-ops typically have down payment requirements that are 25 percent of the purchase price, whereas condos are generally about 30 percent more. "If you have limited resources in terms of cash, but you have good income," says Neil Binder, principal at Bellmarc, a real estate brokerage firm in New York City, "condos might be the only route available to you because of the restrictive equity rules."

There is no minimum equity requirement or down payment in a condominium, but banks will require a minimum equity cash investment or down payment of ten percent as a condition to its lending the remaining 90 percent. In a co-op, the cash requirement limitation is not defined by banks but by a cooperative board (hence the term co-op). Co-op boards have different personalities depending on the city and neighborhood.

Co-ops typically are less transient than condominiums because they don't permit renting. If you want to rent and the ability to sell and buy without any restriction, a condo is a better choice.

Townhouse

Townhouses are nice options and, for many, a good place to start equity. They are always in demand and easily resold.

House versus Apartment

Moving from an apartment to a house usually means added responsibility. If you have been living in a closet of an apartment, you probably haven't dealt extensively with service providers like garbage pickup, phone, and utility companies. One thing is certain: Buying a home will make you very familiar with these organizations!

When moving into a new neighborhood, be prepared to inform everyone you're doing business with.

For example, you'll want to contact your dentist, creditors, professional organizations, attorneys, doctors, tax preparers, and others involved in your care and advancement. Those details can fall through the cracks when you are trying to handle the move yourself.

For instance, you may not think about your voting privilege until you try to vote and realize you haven't registered!

Choosing an Agent

As mentioned earlier, you want your agent to be an ally. To Chaz Walters, choosing an agent is like choosing a doctor. "If you want to have a heart operation," he says, "I'm sure you are going to interview a couple of different surgeons and ask questions. You are not going to let a doctor who only does one open-heart operation a year operate on you." For women living in large cities, finding a real estate agent is as easy as calling most prominent companies and/or those that seem to have a predominant market share. "Many single women do not go into the home buying process with the understanding that the agent's fiduciary responsibility is to the seller unless you have an agent who is listed and has signed an agreement that they are their buyer's agent," says Donna Albrecht.

What this means is that if you mention to a seller's agent that you really like a place and would be willing to pay $5,000 more for it, the agent then is ethically bound to tell the seller that you will pay more money. Instead of a seller's agent, Albrecht recommends getting a buyer's agent or "buyer's broker."

"A buyer's agent or buyer's broker agrees on paper that they will represent your best interest only," she says. In other words, the buyer's agent won't tell the seller that you are willing to pay $5,000 more.

The most important questions to ask when choosing a real estate agent are: How many homes do you sell a month? How long have you been doing this? Where do you rate with the company? Find an agent you can trust, someone who has your best interests in mind for this major life transition.

After you have selected someone you feel fits your needs, it is crucial for you to sit down and discuss what you want out of your property. Technically, the agent should be outlining different concerns specific to your target community and lifestyle issues that will be important to your decision as a single woman. Albrecht says that your agent is not only your home purchasing partner—he or she is also your new link to an entirely fresh experience. "Sometimes there is a tennis club where most of the people are single, but another tennis club might have an awful lot of families and kiddy tournaments," she says. "Your agent can help you find the places in a community where you are going to find the lifestyle that you want most."

Down Payment

The more money you are able to put down, the easier it will be for you to get a loan, and the less the loan will cost you. For example, if you put less than 20 percent down, Private Mortgage Insurance (PMI) is going to be attached to the loan. And based on a $100,000 or $200,000 mortgage, you could be looking at an extra $50 to $180 a month for PMI insurance. Sure, you can eliminate accruing this extra cost by putting 20 percent down, but a lot of first-time home buyers don't have 20 percent.

As a general rule of thumb, banks like to see that people put at least 10 percent down. Sometimes you can go as low as 5 percent down if you go through the Federal Housing Agency (FHA) or Department of Housing and Urban Development (HUD). FHA and HUD provide lenient guidelines by which lenders underwrite prospective homebuyers and properties for risk and loan approval. Lela Leong recalls a client who dealt with this scenario in Los Angeles, which has a down payment assistance program for home buyers. Because she made a moderate to high salary, Leong's client wasn't eligible, but she did win a grant through the Association of Realtors for her down payment. "She was savvy enough to read her real estate section to see what was going on," says Leong. "She found a seminar and won $5,000." Leong adds that most first-time home buyers, regardless of their income levels, can qualify to buy a house with just 3 percent down.

Most major cities also provide down payment assistance to low- and moderate-income buyers through their local housing department. Also check down payment websites in the resource section of this chapter.

The easiest way for single women to save for a down payment is to have a portion of their salary deducted automatically and put into a savings account each month. Women interested in buying a home will need to cut back on expenses so they are better able to put everything toward a down payment. For most, this is a one- or two-year plan. For all, however, it is definitely a challenge.

Women, in general, need to become more disciplined about saving.

Our weakness for saving isn't helped by pressures to have the latest fashions, shoes, accessories, and hairstyles. The simple solution is to cut back on everything and plaster your humble apartment with positive reminders, such as a picture of the house you want. The visuals will help you stay motivated and on target.

Preapproval

For women looking to buy a home, preapproval is sometimes the most important part of the process. You want to make sure you can afford what you are looking for before you even start. With preapproval, sellers may put you at the top of their list. Oftentimes a good real estate agent won't work with you unless you have official confirmation of a lending commitment.

When shopping around for the best bank from which to solicit your preapproval, don't feel pressured to go to the bank where you have your checking accounts. Banks typically enter your criteria into their computers and try to sell you their own loans first before trying to get you the best deal. If you want the best possible deal, go with a mortgage broker; these brokers have anywhere from 200 to 400 investors in their portfolio.

Qualifying for a Mortgage

When deciding whether an individual is qualified for a mortgage, banks use two major criteria.

1. They must see a certain amount of dollars that you plan to contribute. The minimum on a condominium is 10 percent; for a co-op, assuming no restrictions, it's probably 25 percent.

2. No more than 30 percent of your income can be applied to your housing costs. Housing costs are defined as maintenance or common charges, the mortgage payment that you are going to make every month, and in the case of a condo, the real estate taxes that you will also have to pay separately and apart from the common charges. The bank will combine those components and compare this total to your gross income to ensure that the 30 percent requirement is met. When you make the commitment to a loan or a mortgage, you want an institution with a proven service record. Problems can occur if you choose an out-of-state lender or one that doesn't have a proven track record. Ask your agent for help; often he or she can provide some suggestions as to which lender is right for you.

In preparation to meet with a lender, amass all your financial information including taxes, payroll stubs, bank statements, and any other documentation that shows a good payment history. A lender is going to run a credit report on you, so it's best to check your credit report beforehand; problems may show up on a credit report.

Realities of a Mortgage

Not everyone is in a position to purchase a home. Women working in volatile or notoriously unstable industries, such as Internet technology or the performing arts, probably should think twice before signing their lives away. Women who are rarely home should not embark on such a venture. According to Donna Albrecht, "The most important thing to consider is time. How long are you going to be there? And is the timing right in your life for such an important, somewhat exhausting experience? If you are going through a very traumatic personal time, making a major purchase like this may not be in your best interest. You might want to stabilize your personal life a little bit first."

The reality of a mortgage is getting that big bill every month, come rain or shine. If you lose your job, it's up to you to pay. Paying the mortgage can be very stressful, particularly if you're economically thin and just moved into your home.

Buying Your First Home

The key to planning for your first housing purchase is to evaluate the "true costs" associated with buying that particular property. Many women think the true cost is the price stated on the contract. In addition, there are often transfer fees, fixup costs, and furnishings to consider. The true cost of your potential home will be about 10 percent more than the buying price.

Before you sign on that proverbial dotted line, you will spend many hours, days, and months of preparation related to your purchase. Buying a first home means seeing as many properties as possible while simultaneously meeting with and talking to real estate agents and mortgage bankers and brokers to get prequalified.

After you determine what you want to buy, your agent will begin negotiations, and an inspection of the home will take place. Generally, people ask for a five-day attorney approval and home inspection. The mortgage process is then put into motion, and a walk-through is scheduled before the closing takes place. Chazz Walters says that for the first-time buyer, this can be a stressful process. But really, "It's pretty easy," he says. "It's not as hard as everybody thinks. It is nerve-racking, but really it's just like buying a car."

Tips for First–Time Home Buyers

1. *Find the apartment/property that best fits your needs.* Don't look just based on price. Ask yourself about the location, the building and space first, then consider price.

2. *Use a real estate attorney, not a friend.* Real estate lawyers know the law and will be your best resource. Ask for recommendations. Use an attorney who has handled closings in the area so he or she will know about the particulars of the deal.

3. *Try to buy as much as you can afford, regardless of what kind of property it is.* The more one can afford, the greater the appreciation. For singles specifically, this not only makes sense, but it's more feasible. "We can eat less," says Leong. "We don't have to worry about feeding a kid. If I wanted to just eat cottage cheese for a week, I could do that and put more toward my housing payment, which I don't look at as merely shelter. It is an investment."

4. *Use a real estate broker/agent you like.* Make sure your broker is someone who can empathize with you, relate to you, and with whom you can enjoy the experience of buying a home. Ask friends or your loan officer for a referral to someone who will match your personality. Interview the broker as if you were interviewing someone for a job. After all, he or she is helping you with the largest purchase of your life.

5. *Expect things to go wrong.* It should be part of your expectations that things will not be simple. Don't let it get you down.

6. *Never forget that* you *write the check.* Do not be afraid to walk away. You will never lose money on a deal you don't sign. If you are going to buy a home, you should feel comfortable with your decision.

7. *Research, research, research.* Make sure you know enough to accomplish everything you are looking for and decide what is most important to you.

8. *Know as much as you can about the process.* Understanding the financial process is crucial. Do your homework!

Resources

Websites

www.coldwellbanker.com

www.realtor.com

www.hud.gov

Books

Buying a Home When You're Single by Donna Albrecht (John Wiley & Sons, 2001)

Fannie Mae's "*A Guide to Homeownership*": Costs about $1 at *www.fanniemae.com*

The Ultimate Guide to Buying and Selling Co-ops and Condominiums in New York City by Neil Binder (Nice Idea Publishing, 2001)

Sample of Down Payment Assistance Programs

California

www.hud.gov/local/sfc/bafthdap.html

www.caprops.com/homebuyer.html

www.ci.long-beach.ca.us/hdc/programs/downpayment_assistance.htm

Colorado

www.ci.boulder.co.u/hshhs/homeownership/downpaymentasst.htm

New York

www.freddiemac.com

www.homepath.com

www.nw.org

www.wnylc.com

www.nychome.org

www.fanniemaefoundation.org/grants

Pennsylvania

www.pmc_pa.com/purcfir1.html

Seattle, Washington

www.homesightwc.org

www.hud.gov/local/sea/seahmbuy.html

Texas

www.ci.dallas.tx.us/html/home_buyer_assistance_programs.html

....

CHAPTER 6

Tools of the Beauty Trade

City Beauty versus Country Beauty

In the big city, you'll need access to lots of makeup and designer clothing to wear to the many ritzy events you're invited to. But even when you're walking to the corner deli or driving one block to the 7-Eleven you'll want to look your best, in case you run into a handsome city slicker looking oh so *GQ*!

You don't have to worry about looking like a fashionista in rural areas because everyone's wearing overalls and the competition isn't so steep.

The good news is that all of the beauty tools you need lie in wait in big cities. The advantages of living in a big city include accessibility to makeup artists who can do a makeover for you and introduce you to new colors. A disadvantage is that we have so much to choose from that it can be overwhelming. Often we don't know what to choose because we are inundated with cosmetic products by different manufacturers, brands, and designers. We all have little cosmetic stores in our homes! It's time to clean out. Dump all of your cosmetics on an outspread newspaper, sift through, throw away that which is old, keep what's good, and then decide what you need going forward.

Check the expiration data of all products. If the product is odoriferous or has changed in color or texture, toss it. When it smells, it means bacteria are present. Use this handy guide to determine when to discard cosmetics:

Mascara, eyeliner, eye shadow after three months

Lipstick, foundation, powder after six months

Moisturizer, shower gel, shampoo, and sunscreen after one year.

While you're at it, change your attitude toward makeup from one of concern to nonchalance, like celebrities.

Celebrity Stories

Kimara Ahnert, a makeup artist and owner of Kimara Makeup and Skincare Studios in Manhattan, has worked with many celebrities. Most are blasé about makeup.

"They are on their cell phone or going through their Rolodex for their appointments while you are putting their makeup on," says Ahnert.

When she's done with their makeup, the stars don't even look in the mirror.

"They say thank you. Then they go under the camera, do the shoot, and then they run out," she says.

But there are special occasions that affect every single woman, even celebrities.

Ahnert did makeup for Catherine Zeta-Jones's wedding.

"We did a trial beforehand at her apartment. It was very important that she had the look that she wanted for her wedding. She was excited and anxious just like every other bride would be," Ahnert said.

Affording Cosmetics

The average amount women should spend on cosmetics per month is about $25, says Ahnert. Set aside $5 per week in an envelope labeled "cosmetics." At the end of the month, treat yourself to a few new things.

And why not get the expertise of a makeup artist with an upscale cosmetics manufacturer without buying their expensive cosmetics? Simply make an appointment with a top-notch makeup artist at a department store, buy the obligatory one product, and take the written tips home. The makeup artist usually writes out everything she used on you. If you like what you see in the mirror, you can find the colors cheaper at the drugstore.

In addition to drugstores, you can buy cosmetics duty-free when you're traveling abroad to the Caribbean or Europe. Also look for upscale brands, such as MAC and Elizabeth Arden, in discount stores, such as Costco. The problem with cosmetics sold at discount warehouses is that they are in sealed packages, preventing you from seeing how the color looks on your skin. You're taking a chance that the color may not look as good on you as it does on the package. Test out colors in department stores before heading to the discount rack. You can hit various cosmetic counters at department stores for samples. For example, Chanel and Prescriptives give good samples in easy-to-carry jars. Switch up department stores so that you don't run into the same cosmetic clerk when you need a refill!

Shopping at Flea Markets

The advantage of flea markets is that you can find high-end cosmetics for as cheap as $1 to $5. The disadvantage is that the product could be expired. If, for example, a foundation gives you a bad skin reaction, you don't have any recourse because you bought it through a channel that is not company-approved.

Before purchasing at flea markets, check the expiration date. With creams, skin care, foundations, and mascara, you have to be particular because you don't want to get a rash or eye infection that will keep you from looking your most stunning. When dealing with open bins of lipgloss and mascaras, make sure they come with a protective seal; otherwise it may have been used or returned.

But you're safe buying powdered eye shadows that are discounted because they have a much longer shelf life than creams and foundations. The same goes for pencils, lip liners, and brow liners. One good drugstore brand is Wet 'N' Wild. They make stunning eyeshadows.

Drugstore Cosmetics

We tend to spend too much for what we're tangibly getting in return for how it makes us feel. Women are willing to pay for nice packaging because it completes the process of beauty. Remember, though, that the product isn't going to be any better when you buy from Macy's rather than your local drugstore.

"It's the packaging, the fragrance, the commissions, the physical places that you purchase it that is more expensive and adds to the cost of the product. It's not necessarily the product itself," says Lily Kimmel, cosmetics director of Juva MediSpa in Manhattan.

Drugstore cosmetics, such as Cover Girl's Outlast Lip Color in Berry, was proven to outlast pricier Chanel's Infrarouge Lipstick in Pretty, according to the August 2001 issue of *Marie Claire* magazine. Best of all: Cover Girl Berry costs $9.50 while Chanel's Pretty costs $21.50! But of course, who wants to be seen flashing Cover Girl lipstick in the ladies' room at a chic charity event? A happy medium is Origins' Lasting Lip Color in Berry. Not too cheap and not too expensive, it costs $12.

Drugstores buy direct from manufacturers such as Maybelline and Revlon, which makes cosmetics purchased in drugstores no different from those found in department stores. But you won't find high-end brand cosmetics like Borghese or Lancôme at the drugstore!

When it comes to fragrance, the more you pay, the better of a smell you'll get. We all know there's a big difference between Charlie and

Chanel! But as far as cosmetics go, you can feel comfortable purchasing a lipstick, eye shadow, lip liner, and eyeliner in a drugstore.

You also don't want to stock up on too much makeup, especially mascara, because it becomes dated fast.

Affording Clothes

The women's fashion industry tries to convince us that we have to buy the latest fashion every year. A much better approach would be to take a basic item, such as a red dress, and accessorize it with current fashionable scarves, belts, shoes, handbags, earrings, and the like. Subsequently, you're building a wardrobe as opposed to throwing out an old one and starting fresh every season.

When you go clothes shopping, set a realistic budget and buy clothes that you can wear a number of ways. Don't be tempted by sale price alone. Some women will buy an orange dress that matches nothing in their closet just because it's on sale for $30. But once they get the orange dress home, they realize they don't have shoes or a purse to match and they never wear it. There goes $30 down the drain. Or worse, they buy new shoes, a scarf, and a purse to match for $150, negating the sale price.

"The other thing is you want pieces that can be worn more than one season. Three seasons is the best," says Betsy Thompson, fashion spokesperson at Talbots in Hingham, Massachusetts. Clothes that last more than one season typically are classic styles. They can last generations.

Classics include a great white shirt, straight black skirt, pearls, an indispensable white t-shirt, and gray flannel trousers. The beauty of the classic style is that it is timeless. You always look current without having to chase every trend.

Accessorize with current fashions, such as the postman bag, the tassel pump, kitten-heel boots, the wrist clutch, and double-buckle leather belts, to name a few.

"One of the fashion houses that has always worked on that is Nicole Miller, which starts with a basic fashion and over a period of years builds the wardrobe based on one or two new outfits per year so that you don't have to throw everything out," says Mark Neckes, associate professor of marketing at Johnson & Wales University in Miami, Florida.

Other designers that follow this pattern include Donna Karan, Liz Claiborne, and Ralph Lauren.

....

Example

Laura Elwood, a Boston native, has shopped at thrift shops, designer resale shops, sales, and outlets. You name it; she's done it.

"I'm a regular at Filene's Basement, Marshall's, and TJ Maxx," she said. "I look in odd places, like vintage secondhand stores and I'll find weird things. But people always say that I have the most amazing clothes."

The twenty-six-year-old airline stewardess saw a beautiful off-white coat in Neiman Marcus that cost $550. Sadly, she had to leave it on the racks because she couldn't afford it.

A few months later, she saw the exact same coat at Filene's and bought it for $35. She spent an additional $75 to have it tailored.

"It was worth it," she said. The petite blonde recently bought a Diane Von Furstenburg silk dress for $22, also at Filene's. "You have to be there on the right day. You have to hunt," she said.

....

Elwood is like many single women who live in big cities and jump on a bargain. It's not bad to shop for bargains, but make sure it's something you can use.

Rather than getting caught up in the moment, change your frenzied perception of a sale to "There's another sale coming."

Consider a major sale as an opportunity to add one or two things to your wardrobe that you may want to try out but don't want to spend a fortune on. Perhaps you want to try a fun color, such as bright fuchsia pink. But make sure that it goes with something else in your closet so that you're not forced to buy accessories for it. When you are discount shopping, be aware of the return policy at the store. Ask what the policy is before purchasing anything.

Be wary of buying without having tried it on first. If it doesn't fit and you can't get your money back, it doesn't matter what the sale price is. You wasted your money because you can't wear it. Save the day by swapping clothes with a girlfriend who does fit into the outfit.

It's easy to get excited about finding a Kate Spade bag at a discount store, but how do you know it's not a knockoff? The way to know quality is to go into the expensive department stores (the Gallerias, the Saks Fifth Avenues, the Lord and Taylors, the Neiman Marcuses) and study the designer items. That way you'll know the real thing when you come across it shopping at outlets and sample sales.

If it seems too cheap to be true, then it probably is!

A Bargainizer's Glossary

As is—In current condition; all sales are final.

Closeout—The item will no longer be made or sold.

High end or low end—Describes quality and workmanship— high end being more expensive.

In-season—Current styles offered by season.

Manufacturer's outlet—Items directly from the manufacturer.

Overrun—Extra merchandise available after the retailers have filled their orders.

Retail—The usual price in retail stores; includes the store's markup over the manufacturer's price.

Returns—New merchandise the retailer has returned because it arrived too late.

Sample—The marketing representative's example used to sell orders to volume buyers.

Seconds—Items with some type of flaw that affects the overall quality or look.

Wholesale—The price the retailer pays on quantity orders of merchandise. Retailers generally mark up items 50 percent over wholesale.

Smart Shopping Tips

- Try eBay. The website offers discounted designer clothes. One woman reported buying a pair of DKNY jeans for $8—but beware of knockoffs.

- Ask a salesperson at your favorite chain or department store when the next sale items will be put out.

- Ask a salesperson to set aside outfits for you before the shop doors open on the day of the sale.

- If they've run out of a marked-down item in your size at a popular outlet, call another outlet across town to see if they have it available.

Thrift Shopping

Oh, the thrill of finding a great item at a fabulous price! It's fun! But what about the morning after, when you don the dress and discover a stain that wasn't there the day before? Look for stains, tears, and loose threads before making the purchase. Also, have

---

Designer Clothes Shopping on **eBay.com**

To bid on auctions, you have to become an eBay member and sign up with *www.paypal.com*. That electronic payment service makes shopping on eBay easier because most sellers accept it.

Registering for *www.paypal.com* can be cumbersome, but it's free. Most sellers also take money orders; only a few take Visa.

Once you're all set to pay, use the eBay search engine to help find what you need. For example, type in "Gucci women's pants" to see what's available.

Check out shipping charges with the seller before bidding on any item because some charge a flat rate, which can be high. It's always good to review feedback on the seller. Normally, a link on the seller is posted with the auction item.

Another thing to check is sizing. If it's not listed, ask about it because most sales are final, and there is nothing worse than spending money on something that doesn't fit and that you can't return.

Patricia Handschiegel, 30, has purchased Earl jeans, three pairs of Chinese laundry shoes, a Vivienne Tam suit, two Custo tops, two pairs of Guess pants, an Express sweater, and Frankie B jeans in five months!

---

access to a good seamstress because you may need to have some things altered.

Sample Sales

Although sample sales can be great places to find designer clothes at a discount, the main disadvantage is limited size offerings, which can be disappointing for women over a certain size.

The typical misses' size is between 6 and 10, depending on the designer. The more expensive and popular the designer, the smaller the size that you fit into. For example, you may be a size 10 but be able to fit into a size 8 or 6.

"The reason for that is if you're going to spend that money, you might as well feel good about getting into a smaller size," says Mark Neckes.

Bear in mind, too, that generally sample sale items are not returnable. Another thing to look out for is that the garment doesn't have a lot of wear and tear or that the fit has not been altered. Always try on clothing at sample sales before shelling out cash.

Often a sample is cut for a model who is very tall. If you buy it thinking that you can have it altered, keep in mind that sometimes alterations cost as much as the outfit itself. If you have to completely restructure the garment, it might not be worth the cost.

Outlet Shopping

Don't assume you're getting a bargain in an outlet store—because you may not be.

Know the actual prices of things because sometimes items at outlets aren't priced so low. Expect discounts of 30 and 40 percent off what the regular price would be. Some designers manufacture strictly for outlet shops so the merchandise is not necessarily coming from a designer shop to the outlet.

Before shopping at outlets, price the merchandise at designer shops so that you know you're getting a good value.

Apparel Marts

Apparel marts are more difficult to finagle than outlets. You can't walk right into a manufacturer unless you know someone or have

---

Tips for Shopping at Outlets

- Come prepared with a list of items you are looking for. This will help you not spend money on things you don't need.

- Keep in mind that outlet stores are owned and operated by the designers and brands—the salespeople in the outlet stores work directly for the brands. (Author's note: They may not be objective.)

- Sign up for the mailing lists of your favorite stores to be notified of special sales and promotions.

- Check the center's website to see if it offers any information on sales and promotions. For example, *www. PremiumOutlets.com* lists sales and promotions and also has an online VIP Shopper Club for added savings and center updates.

- Request a map from the outlet. That way you have your game plan before arriving. Some outlets offer maps on their website.

Source: Michele Rothstein, vice president of marketing, Chelsea Premium Outlets

---

an invitation. Apparel marts have sales of sample merchandise once or twice a year, but the general public doesn't hear about it. If it's advertised in the paper, it's not really an apparel mart sale. Cultivate a connection at the apparel mart in your city, or better yet, take a part-time job there! You'll make money while you shop and get a discount.

Internet

The Internet makes it easier to comparison-shop and to study designer labels from home. Instead of having to pound the pavement, you can check prices from the comfort of your own home. You also can do a search to see what's on sale before setting out for your monthly shopping excursion.

"The Internet can be a great benefit. If you are going out shopping, it's a good idea to use the Internet to see what the retail value is so then you can really gauge whether you're getting a good deal or not," says Betsy Thompson.

Hair Salon Freebies

....

Example

Loretta Swen is a struggling actress. She pounds the pavement in Manhattan with a Coach backpack purse slung over her back that she bought for $200 at a designer resale shop on the Upper East Side. Wearing Theory pants and a matching black jacket, she looks like she just walked out of a magazine ad.

The slim cigarette-smoker lives for the day that NYPD Blue *will call again. She's already appeared on the show three times in bit parts.*

No one would ever know that she's two months behind in her rent by the way she's groomed. Her golden hair is always freshly cut, blow-dried, and highlighted even though she can barely pay the rent for her West 106th Street walk-up. Her secret? She frequents class night at upscale hair salons in Manhattan.

....

Among the salons that offer free or discounted hair services in big cities, such as Manhattan, are Frederic Fekkai and Louis Licari. Louis Licari of Manhattan offers free blow-dries on class nights, which are Wednesdays at 5:30 P.M., but only if a beginning assistant hasn't mastered blow-dries.

"It's not like every single week whoever wants a complimentary blow-dry can come in, but when we have a new assistant start in the cutting department we look for people who want a nice little blow-dry," says Kimberly Brown, salon manager at Louis Licari.

During class nights, the salon charges $40 for single hair color process, $60 for highlights, $75 for single plus highlight, and $30 for haircuts. Services at these prices are a steal. Any woman who colors her hair knows that single process highlights can cost $175 and more at pricey city salons.

With free or discounted hair services given by students, there's always the chance that you won't like what's done to your hair. In that case, call the manager the following day and let him or her know exactly what you're not happy with.

Class night at these salons don't take everyone. If your hair is in very bad condition, you will be rejected.

Also, don't expect to pop in and out within forty-five minutes on class night. A simple blow-dry can take two hours rather than the standard forty-five minutes. It's a learning experience for the students. You might get lucky and fall into the hands of an experienced student who has been blow-drying for a year. But then again, you could wind up with an assistant who's just starting out. Most of the time, salons won't allow you to request a particular assistant.

Cutting takes about two to three hours, coloring can take more than three hours, and highlights range from three to four hours. To find hair salons that offer free or discounted classes, call salons in your city at least four to six weeks in advance or check the resource list in the Appendix.

CHAPTER 7

....

Movin' On Up

City Women versus Country Women

This chapter will help working girls wind up at the top of the corporate pole so that they can afford the finer things in life.

Single women living in urban areas have the capacity to earn
more money because there are more opportunities in big cities.
Women in big cities tend to be very competitive and aggressive
because they've learned that that is the only way to get ahead.

Urban women have a better chance at success than women in
small towns, where there aren't as many corporate jobs. Cities are
much more progressive when it comes to women's rights. Don't
be surprised if you're labeled "little lady" in small Southern towns.

On the downside, in metropolitan areas there are more societal
pressures around what you do for work. The pressure makes single
women in urban settings much more ambitious than their suburban counterparts. It also quickens the pace of working and creates
a sense of urgency about moving their careers along toward success.

The catch is that it's more difficult to move up in big cities
because the competition is much more intense. This chapter will
give ideas on how to maneuver your way into the corner office
with a view and a big, overstuffed chair.

Disparity Between Men and Women on the Job

Women in big cities face a higher cost of living. While men have the same challenge, they often make more money to meet it.

"Despite the disparity, women are still expected to dress the same and pay for the same lunch expenses and travel expenses on a lower salary," says Cynthia Fico Simpson, human resource director at *BeliefNet.com* in Manhattan.

Facts about Women and Their Money

- Women earned only about 76 cents for every dollar that men earned overall in 1999, according to the U.S. Department of Labor.
- Women make up 46 percent of the workforce.
- Half of all women who work in traditionally female, low-paying jobs are without pensions, according to the Women's Institute for a Secure Retirement in Washington.
- Three out of four working women earn less than $30,000 a year and nine out of ten earn less than $40,000 a year.

The fact is that Joe in the cubicle next to you probably makes more money. Before you blow your stack about it, consider this advice. When you find out that a male colleague is being paid more, try to find out:

- If you have the same educational background
- If you have the same skills
- If you have the same kind of prior work history

If all of these things measure up equally, engage the human resources department and your management in a discussion.

"The worst thing is when somebody comes to me and says, 'Joe is being paid more than I am and we have the same job.' I dig a little bit deeper and find out that it's not true. You end up opening a can of worms," Simpson said.

Another thing you don't want to do is to show your anger.

There are many ways to put issues on the table, but getting mad is not a good way. Manage your anger until you can rectify the situation. Until then, call a powwow with your girlfriends to vent about the injustices of your world.

Finding a Corporate Job

If you're itching to get into an aggressively paying corporate environment, search the Internet for job postings, talk with job agencies and headhunters, network at industry functions, and consider a graduate degree. Having an MBA or other graduate degree can make a difference in your salary and title. Candidates with an MBA probably will be paid more than the ones without because they come to the table with a richer understanding of business.

Salary

The key to getting a bigger salary is finding out how much other people are earning for the same work. That's where professional organizations come in handy. People are more likely to talk about their salaries away from their place of employment, such as at professional events. That doesn't mean asking everyone's salary at a cocktail reception but rather inquiring about different positions at other companies and what those positions pay.

When considering salaries, take into consideration the company size and visit *www.Salary.com* to see what your market rate should be. The site lists different job titles, professions, and salary ranges.

Depending on how much experience you have, place yourself low, medium, or high. If you're new in the industry, you'll be at the low end of the salary range. If you're seasoned, have years of experience, an MBA, or specialized expertise, you'll be at the high end of the range.

Once you determine your job's salary range, you can take the information to your boss or human resources department and explain why you should be on the upper end of the range.

Another way to find out whether you are being underpaid is by interviewing with other companies for similar positions.

New Ways to Get a Salary Increase

If, in your research, you discover that you are overworked and underpaid, determine your market value, evaluate your skills, and present a recommendation to your manager on what you should be earning. If you're a star player or key employee in the company, a manager usually will fight to get you a bigger salary.

"When a manager sells the concept of giving somebody an increase, it makes it easier for me because usually I've noticed when somebody needs an increase. I know who in the database is not being paid market value," says Simpson.

Rather than wasting energy complaining about not being paid enough, keep track of your own performance. Nowadays employees own their career and they are responsible for it. No longer is the company going to move you along and help shape your career. You have to shape it the same way you tweeze your eyebrows once a week.

If you opt to appeal to human resources, have a list prepared of at least five or six reasons why you personally need an increase. HR director Simpson advises bringing in performance examples and a written self-evaluation.

Another outdated model is expecting a salary increase with an annual review. Many companies are moving away from that, which means that workers have to start fighting for their increases. Doing this requires that you keep notes about your own performance, accomplishments, lessons learned, and skills throughout the year.

From there you can use your notes to recommend an increase for yourself.

Once you're in an organization, it can be difficult to get a big salary increase because there are ranges of increments that are standard. But if you're asked to take on an expanded assignment, it's a good excuse to ask for a substantial increase.

"Annual increases are decided based on the budget. The manager may have discretion about how they are distributed. Asking for a raise close to distribution time is probably not the best idea. It's best to lay the groundwork earlier," says Karen Metzger, a career counselor in New York. You lay the groundwork by keeping copious notes of your accomplishments and progress.

Examine Your Job Skills

Take a skills inventory by asking yourself these questions:

- What have I done at my current job?
- What have I developed?
- What has been the result of using some of these skills?
- Which skills are transferable to other industries and companies?
- What am I passionate about?
- What aspect of my job do I hate?

Look back at the past three months to see what you've accomplished. Notice the responsibilities that you set aside because you don't enjoy them. The skills you put off are the ones to hone.

On the Internet, look at job postings, which will tell you what skill sets companies are looking for. From that list you'll know what makes you more marketable or less marketable. Professional associations can keep you abreast of what's hot in your industry. If you're in marketing, you can join the Direct Marketing Association or the American Marketing Association. If you're in promotions, join the Promotional Society of America.

Association meetings also provide networking opportunities. Their newsletters and other industry publications are often great sources of information on popular skills.

Your most marketable skills are the ones that you are most passionate about. The projects that you are excited about are the ones that you should seek out when you're looking for a new position.

Job Titles

A title can make or break you in the professional and social world. The higher your title, the more respect you get. What comes with a title is formal power, which gives you authority. Higher titles allow you access to certain people, information, and meetings.

A title may not bring you more money but it can make you eligible for another level of benefits. "It creates a perceived level of credibility with outside clients, and it gives you advantages in terms of compensation and perks," says Nancy Friedberg, president of Career Leverage, a career-counseling firm in Manhattan.

A director gets more attention than a coordinator because the director is perceived as the decision maker. Internally, without a title, you don't get the recognition or respect you deserve. Never mind that you work harder than the manager or director; you still won't get respect.

So, how do you go from associate to director?

The best way to negotiate a higher title is to ask for the most important title you can get while you are interviewing for a new job; often it's a negotiable item when you're getting hired.

If you're not happy with your current title, begin looking outside for a position that's suitable to your current skill level or work with your current manager on a new title within the company.

Within an existing job, find out what standards of performance would make you eligible for consideration for the next title. Start to exceed those standards so that you have the basis to ask for the new title.

In the meantime, pull up job descriptions from the Internet that match your skill set, print them out, and show them to your boss, saying "Look at the three different titles I've discovered on the Internet. They all have the same responsibilities that I do but the title is vice president rather than associate."

Potential for Promotion

A promotion is often our only means of making the money we need to shop and groom ourselves, but getting a promotion is about as hard as getting an engagement ring.

Look up from your desk, gaze across the horizon of cubicles, and study reality. Is there room to grow at your place of employment? For example, if you have one manager ahead of you, how long has he or she been there? If she's just been promoted, that person probably isn't going anywhere any time soon, which means you're stuck. You might want to look for growth opportunities elsewhere.

If your goal is to move from manager to director and the director has staff while you don't, how can you prepare for a promotion if nobody is reporting to you? Go to your manager and explain that you are trying to become a director. Ask if the department assistant or intern can report to you so that you can get some management experience.

Groom yourself for the promotion by doing the job beforehand.

Talk to your manager about your goals. List your accomplishments in the past nine to twelve months and get feedback. Ask point-blank: What would it take for me to get to the next level?

If the boss thinks that you haven't been performing as well as you think you have, then go back to the drawing board and work on the areas that are lagging. The last resort is to find a better job or start your own business. (See Chapter 8.)

Six Signs You're on the Fast Track

1. You are being kept in the loop.

2. You get invited to critical meetings.

3. You are on all the important distribution lists for information.

4. You've been promoted in the past.

5. You're assigned high-visibility projects.

6. You're recognized either outwardly or subtly.

If you're not being promoted and you want to stay with your company, you may want to get 360-degree feedback through an outside executive coach. "360-degree" feedback is when someone collects data on you and assesses your performance based on managers', staff members', and bosses' perceptions.

You then receive a feedback report, with which you can put together a development plan that helps you to see strengths, weaknesses, obstacles, and blind spots.

In the absence of 360-degree feedback, find a way to solicit feedback. Subtly ask those most influential in managing your career. In addition, start a PR campaign about yourself.

"If you see somebody important on the elevator, use the opportunity to talk about a big project you completed that saved the company $50,000. See it as a fifteen-second infomercial about yourself or a more subtle way of marketing your accomplishments," Nancy Friedberg says.

Another way to make yourself promotable is to make yourself important outside the office in your industry. If you're a member of the National Secretary's Association, why not run for president? Or write an article for an important industry publication and pass it on to key people in your company. Outside activity improves credibility and visibility. Just as it is in high school with extracurricular activities, so it is on the job. Your value goes up when the external world validates you.

In other words, you have to manage the perception that you're doing good work. Don a marketing hat and start talking about yourself! Marketing to promote your career is an ongoing process.

Get out and network! Pick ideas from the minds of people in other companies and then bring them back to your job. You'll gain leverage as a source of information.

Make the most of your job by thinking of it as doing a service for the universe. Become indispensable. Offer assistance in other areas, offer to learn, ask questions, and ask for new responsibilities. Be an innovator. Come up with suggestions, ideas, and alternative ways of doing things.

Job Hopping

Stay at least one to two years with an employer before moving on. Most managers and human resources professionals frown on people going from job to job every six months to a year because they value loyalty. By the same token, staying too long with a firm raises eyebrows as well. Five years is way too long unless you're already at the top of the heap, especially if you're doing the exact same thing for five years.

If you're not happy, start looking for a new job after you've been there one year. It will take at least six months for you to find a better position, which will give you an acceptable year and a half at the hated firm.

If you're a notorious job-hopper looking to make good with a potential new employer, make it clear why you changed employers. The worst thing is being apologetic for why you hopped. You don't want the potential employer to think that you have bad judgment, which may well be the case!

Thirteen Signs that You've Outgrown Your Job

1. You're bored.

2. You don't feel challenged.

3. You no longer gain satisfaction from your work.

4. You take longer lunches then usual.

5. You hate Monday mornings.

6. You're having trouble getting out of bed every day of the week.

7. You find yourself often daydreaming.

8. You are easily distracted.

9. You're burned out.

10. You feel stagnant or stuck in a rut.

11. You are eating and drinking alcohol in larger amounts than usual.

12. You frequently make mistakes in your work.

13. You're depressed.

Five Signs that You're about to Be Fired

1. You're being excluded from important meetings.

2. Your boss avoids you.

3. You're not getting good assignments.

4. Colleagues are creating distance.

5. You feel that you are out of the information loop.

When All Else Fails

In some cases, you can smile until your face hurts, schmooze until you run out of breath, and shake hands until your arm falls off, but you know deep in your heart you've reached what's called the "glass ceiling," meaning that you can look up and see that level above you but are unable to get there. You've learned everything there is to know about the business. Heck, you can run it yourself, but the powers that be won't let you. Why should they? It's not your business! You've reached the last house on the block. The only thing left to do is start your own. The next chapter will help you to do just that.

Resources

Creative Negotiating: Proven Techniques for Getting What You Want from Any Negotiation by Stephen Kozicki (Adams Media Corporation, June 1998)

Directory of National Trade and Professional Associations of the United States by J. Valerie Eele (Columbia Books, February 2000)

The 5 O'Clock Club, a national career counseling organization, 1-800-538-6645 ext. 600 or *www.fiveoclockclub.com*

Targeting the Job You Want by Kate Wendleton and Wendy Rothman (Career Press, 2001)

www.careerjournal.com

www.careers.org

www.Salary.com

CHAPTER 8

....

Big Bucks for Businesswomen

Women are leaving corporate America at twice the rate of men. One of the most compelling reasons is that they want to start their own businesses. More than ever before, women with executive-level experience want more autonomy and control.

Corporate women often feel they've hit a roadblock or a glass ceiling in the corporate world. Other times they simply have a passion and a drive for something they want to do themselves. Women realize that when they work for an employer, they are working to enrich someone besides themselves, says Elizabeth Carlassare, author of *Dot Com Divas.* "When you have your own business," she says, "you have the potential to receive the benefit of the profits."

Five Reasons Why Women Start Businesses

1. They feel like they have a good idea.

2. Doing so provides an opportunity to do work that is more valued than what they are currently doing in a corporate job.

3. They perceive it as an opportunity to make more money.

4. By starting their own business, they'll gain more flexibility so that they might enjoy their lives.

5. They have reached the glass ceiling in corporate jobs.

Benefits of an Urban-based Business

One of the major benefits to owning an urban business is the network of contacts you have at your disposal. There are a lot of people who can help you get your business off the ground. For example, in California's Silicon Valley—likely the most famous start-up region in the United States—there is an eclectic mix of entrepreneurs, technologists, angel investors, mentors, and venture capitalists at your disposal.

Another benefit to businesses in urban areas is the specific location advantage afforded to their owners. Like real estate, location is everything. In the ultimate metropolis of Manhattan, for example, you have the flexibility to offer services that fit a wide variety of specific needs, such as a dog-walking service or a store that sells only lampshades. "Critical mass," says Greg Fairchild, a professor at the University of Virginia's Darden Graduate School of Business Administration, is the key and "one aspect of why cities have become great areas for women-owned businesses."

For urban women specifically, says Jamie Wyrick, founder and president of the Forum for Women Entrepreneurs in Fort Worth, Texas, the potential to meet customer needs is much greater because, simply, there are more customers in cities. "You create a business because there is a problem and you want to solve it and that means there is an opportunity there," says Wyrick. "And when there are lots of opportunities, there tends to be more businesses started."

Downsides to city businesses are that labor and property costs are going to be higher, so renting the physical office space that you need is going to be more expensive than it would be if you were starting a business in a suburban area.

Self-Employed versus Business

Many single women are opting to be self-employed free agents where they are sole proprietors because it offers supreme flexibility. They work for themselves or they contract out some expertise or service that they offer.

Self-employment and growing a full-fledged corporation are two different approaches to becoming a business owner.

"A consulting practice is more of a lifestyle type of business, whereas growing a company is more for building equity," says Jean Stafford, founder of Executive Coaching for Women.

In addition to flexibility, self-employment (or sole proprietorship) offers self-accountability. However, being a sole proprietor limits your options because the business is *you*. Starting a larger business with employees gives you a much larger profit potential because you can sell it later on down the line.

"A lot of entrepreneurs prefer going the bigger business route to have that scalability and growth potential so they can go in with the hope and ambition that this might be something that they can sell off five or ten years down the road and retire," says Elizabeth Carlassare. "With a sole proprietorship, you'll have flexibility and autonomy, but you won't necessarily have the ability to sell the business at a huge profit."

How Business Creates Wealth

Clearly, when you own your own business, there is no ceiling on your earnings. The flip side is you have to make it a profitable company in order to have money to control. There is also the chance to build equity and sell the company, which is something you couldn't do working for somebody else.

Entrepreneurship is one of the top three ways to become wealthy in this country, second to investments and occupation.

Selling your business involves not only valuing it, but finding and connecting to purchasers who would have the interest and income to buy it.

A number of venture capital (VC) firms invest in women-owned businesses, and some networking organizations connect VCs to women business owners. Doing so helps people find new businesses, and people find ways to sell their businesses. (See Resources at end of chapter for a list of women VCs.)

••

Example

From the day she started out in public relations as a young professional, Binay Cahn had dreamed of owning her own business. Her father was an independent drugstore owner when she was a child, which influenced Binay's decision to strike out on her own.

The thirty-one-year-old worked at various PR firms for ten years until she felt ready to manage her own clients. Today she is president and CEO of Galaxy Six Strategies, a public relations and media training firm in San Francisco.

After one year of operation, Binay has a couple of people working for her on an independent-contractor basis.

Motivating herself to take the plunge was a no-brainer. "It was really fun for me to be able to explore areas such as accounting or working with a designer for my own business cards, creating your own logo. That was the exciting part," she says.

Her initial investment was buying a computer for $500. Then Binay began the process of selecting clients. She has only three clients at any given time, including those in the consumer, technology, finance, Internet, and publishing industries.

"In retrospect, there were some clients that I didn't take on because I was nervous about the amount of work that we were assuming. I wanted to grow at a steady pace," she says.

Choosing clients was partly about whether they would pay for her services, and she made some mistakes in judgment.

"I look back at a couple of clients and think that would have been a nice client to have but I turned them down," she says.

Getting business through meeting and greeting potential clients is the easy part. "The worst part is actually realizing you still have to get your hands dirty by working," she says.

....

Before Going into Business

Women considering starting their own business must carefully weigh their tolerance for risk. For example, often it's much easier to become entrepreneurial if there is a husband in the household who continues to receive a regular paycheck. This security and cushion is usually not available if you're single. So, having enough savings in place until your business becomes profitable is crucial.

What It Takes to Run a Business

- Leadership
- Management skills
- Tenacity
- Vision
- Relationship skills
- Faith
- Tolerance for risk
- Willingness to work hard
- Perseverance
- Willingness to delegate

Five Steps to Start a Business

The Small Business Administration (SBA) is an excellent resource; it has a women's division specifically focused on women starting their own businesses. Organizations like this one and others suggest that a wise first step is to write a business plan that defines the company's mission.

Step 1: Write a business plan. Business plans require that you:

- Define and identify your customers.
- Predict what problems you will solve for these customers.
- Specify how much investment capital you need.
- Specify how it's going to be spent.
- List what kind of cash flow you are anticipating.
- Assess your market positioning.
- Explain the brand.

It's also important to analyze the market niche you are targeting to determine if there is a business worth capturing. If you're in New York, Wyoming, Connecticut, or Arizona, sign up for a free growing-a-profitable-business class at the Workshop in Business Opportunities, a nonprofit organization (*www.wibo.org*).

Step 2: Put your ducks in a row. Take advantage of the free resources available to you during the planning stages *before* you leave whatever security you have to start your own company. Those free resources include the Small Business Development and SCORE offices (which provide resources and counseling) and women business development centers, which offer free reviews of your documents, projections, and target market. (See the resource list at the end of the chapter for contact information.)

Another good resource is the Chamber of Commerce, which offers business classes in some cities. In urban areas, you may have fifteen to twenty different chambers to choose from, so selecting the best one may require research.

Step 3: Create a support network. When you're starting a business, you have nothing more than your passion for what you are trying to achieve and no structure in place. To compensate for this, build up a support network of mentors—people who can help you if you run into a legal problem or have an accounting question, business-related problem, or a marketing inquiry. Ask successful business people to provide their verbal help in your start-up process.

Step 4: Secure the appropriate professionals to advise you. Retain a legal specialist who understands the start-up world. You also will need financial specialists to manage financial documents and strategic sales/marketing and PR specialists.

Step 5: Build up some capital before diving off the deep end into self-employment. Expect to spend thousands of dollars to get a solid company off the ground. "This doesn't mean you can't work from home and do something small over the course of a year or two before you expand up," Stafford says. "But I would never try to launch without $50,000 to $100,000 in the bank, and even that's not going to get you very far." Private investors, such as angels and venture capitalists, can provide the money you need.

Challenge of Starting a Business

Depending on the kind of company you're starting, you may not have a revenue stream immediately. There may be a very large investment of time and money up front. You won't be able to do marketing, sales, or legal work without capital.

Even if your goal is to start small and work from home, at some point the business will have to grow beyond your home, which means you'll need money for office space.

Access to affordable qualified professionals is another challenge. For example, finding appropriate business partners or staff members may be difficult. Many people going into business for the first time may not understand exactly the skill set of getting a start-up up and running. The skills required change as the company develops. In the early stages, most women business owners wear many hats.

Pros of Owning a Business

An obvious pro to owning a business is independence: financially, creatively, and professionally. Women can gain a huge amount of freedom by starting businesses. As a business owner, your destiny is your own.

If you're willing to take the risk, then you get the benefits, but it is a difficult road—especially if you don't have a partner.

Cons of City Businesses

If the upside is freedom, the downside is uncertainty. The psychological battle is finding a way to manage and cope with the fear of the unknown and the stress of worrying. Business Owners Debtor's Anonymous (BDA) can help at *www.danyc.org*.

Another downside is that cities are filled with infrastructural obstacles. If you have a business involving an operation beyond retail, you'll have to contend with codes, regulatory concerns, and inspections. And while cities are great because they attract transitional people who can be hired easily, finding qualified workers who are reliable, trustworthy, and on time is not always so simple. Transitional people are just that: transitional. Your employees may decide to leave within a year or less.

Five Top Pitfalls of City-based Businesses

1. *Lack of customers.* You have to make enough money to stay in business. It doesn't matter how good your services or products are if you don't have customers.

2. *Failure to delegate.* A big mistake women make when starting a business is that they try to do everything by themselves.
You get burned out when you don't delegate.

3. *Lack of an advisory board.* Amass a group of people together
as advisors, no matter what type of business you're starting.
An advisory board can range from lawyers and peer professionals to accountants and strategists.

4. *Not having enough access to capital.* No savings at the beginning means you won't have enough to live on while you wait
for your first paycheck—which could take months.

5. *Lack of a network.* Build a safety net of people to get access
to capital. The richer your network of connections, the better off you'll be in securing financing. A network of potential capital resources, leaders in the community, connected
peers, and potential customers at medium- and Fortune
1000-sized companies will help. You cannot grow a really big
business until you have access to Fortune 1000 companies.

· ·

Example

It's been three years since Mariam Naficy founded Eve.com, *which became
the Web's most successful retailer of cosmetics. Today* Eve.com's *URL is
no longer active, the company is closed, and Mariam is a part-time consultant in San Francisco.*

But she is anything but a dot.com casualty.

Mariam said the evolution of Eve.com *started with a whole lot of brain-
storming. "The start-up ideas I had were Internet and non-Internet
related," she says. "Then I changed my mind and worked solely on the
Internet idea, the Eve idea, because of what was happening around me and
the easy availability of venture capital."*

Mariam says that getting the money was based on networking. She had been living in the Bay area since 1993 and all the while building up a network of people who knew venture capitalists or were venture capitalists themselves because she knew she was going to start her own business.

"In the first round, we used those contacts as well as contacts from business school," she says. "I had gone to Stanford Business School and my partner had gone to Harvard. So between the two of us we could tap into the alumni database and get introductions to a lot of people. As you probably have heard from others getting venture capital, it is really very much driven by who you know."

Simply sending a business plan to VCs is not enough.

The best way to get a return call from a VC is to be referred by someone the VC knows. The idea is get a first meeting and pitch them directly.

After raising three rounds of financing totaling $28 million, Eve.com was born in July 1998. It took about two years to grow the company, and it consumed all of Mariam's time. "I worked six days a week and sometimes seven. There was a period of time before our launch where I worked two months with not a single day off," she said. "I worked in investment banking prior to starting my business, and I thought that was difficult. Eve.com was a lot longer hours than that."

As a result of her hard work, Mariam and her partner grew the business to about $10 million in annual sales, 2 million unique visitors, 125 employees, and carrying some 200 brands of prestigious department store cosmetics.

Finding a buyer wasn't too difficult. Louis Vuitton-Moët-Hennessy, the luxury goods conglomerate, had been sniffing around. But the two women owners sold Eve.com to Idealab in May 2000 because the incubator had helped the company to grow as silent investors. Idealab shut down Eve.com five months later.

"They were passive, very passive investors," Mariam says about Idealab. "They invested in us in our very first round of financing, and as an existing shareholder, they had a lot of influence on the decision to whom to sell the business to."

Idealab was a "known quantity" and offered more money than Louis Vuitton, an amount Mariam would only say was in the "millions."

It appears Mariam and partner got out just in time before the economy took a turn for the worse. In hindsight, she says there had been signs of a market downturn—mainly that it was becoming harder to secure financing.

"We thought we were doing something wrong. We didn't realize it was the whole market that was changing. We thought that we had lost our magic touch in terms of raising money for the business," she says. "We thought maybe it's time to insure the long-term survival of the company by selling it to a strategic partner. That way, that partner will always fund the business and keep it going."

As a result of selling her business, Mariam enjoys greater financial flexibility.

"I'm very happy the investors and employees were able to make money from our company," she says. "Everyone walked away with a nice financial return, and in the process I think we had fun working together."

The tables have turned for Mariam. Struggling entrepreneurs now see her as a potential investor. They ask her for money to start up their business!

....

Partner Up

Women looking to start their own businesses can benefit greatly from bonding with other women facing the same challenge or with those who have experience running successful enterprises. When getting started for yourself, look to find someone as a mentor who demonstrates the character traits you would like for yourself. Look for a woman who has been there and ask for her help.

Durable Businesses for City Women

The smartest thing you can do for yourself when planning a durable business is to do what you love. Durable means a business that will weather the ups and downs of the economy.

Aim for a business with "scalability." Companies that are venture-fundable companies need to have a scalable revenue model. Trading hours for dollars in a consulting practice is not considered a scalable service because it takes an individual to deliver the service. If, on the other hand, you've got a product, gadget, or technology that doesn't take a person to deliver physically every time, then your service becomes "scalable" because it can reproduce itself and produce a revenue stream over time.

Industries that have seen the most significant growth for women-owned businesses are communications, public utilities, and financial services.

The construction industry has experienced a breakthrough by women in terms of increased growth rates. There was 95 percent growth between 1987 and 1992.

In terms of overall fast-growing areas, service businesses remain number one among women-owned enterprises. They made up about 49 to 55 percent of all women-owned businesses over the last twenty years. A close second business area among women is retail trade, which represented anywhere from 25 percent to as low as 19 percent in the 1982 to 1992 time period.

Resources

Brand Fidelity—Service to address the challenge of creating commercial name and brand: *www.brandfidelity.com*

Business.com: Internet resource for business providing the business news, information, and market insight and leading Web-based services to enable businesspeople to stay informed and competitive.

Business Information Centers—State-of-the-art technology and business software: *www.sba.gov/bi/bics/bicfactsheet.html*

BusinessForSale.com—Search over 12,000 businesses for sale from the United States, United Kingdom, Canada, Australia, South Africa, and 70 other countries.

Calendar of events in your city of SBA seminars and workshops on starting a business: *www.sba.gov/calendar*

CEO partners—Free seminars on marketing: sales, and management: *www.CEOPartners.net*

Federal Business Opportunities: *www.fedbizopps.gov*

FedForms.gov—"one-stop-shopping" for forms needed for the top 500 government services used by the public: *www.fedforms.org*

Franchise Opportunities—Directory of franchises and franchise business services: *www.FranchiseOpportunities.com*

Internal Revenue Service: Small Business and Self Employed Community—Offers industry/profession specific information and provides links to other helpful non-IRS sites: *www.irs.gov/ smallbusiness/index.htm*

My Own Business—A free Internet course on how to start a business: *www.myownbusiness.org*

The National Association of Women's Business Organization (*www.NAWBO.org*) teaches women and small companies how to get access to the corporate world for procurement and contract opportunities.

One-Stop Capital Shops—In Empowerment Zones/Enterprise Communities: *www.sba.gov/onestop*

SCORE—Provides resources and counseling services online: *www.score.org*

Seed Corp Business Plan Booklet: *www.seedcorp.com*

The Small Business Assistance Center (SBAC) provides a "free," half hour office consultation to those of you who are just getting your business started. Discussions can include legal and tax matters, funding, insurance, etc.: *www.sbacnetwork.org*

Small Business Development Centers—Help to get started and grow successfully: *www.sba.gov/sbdc*

Telejunctions.com: Free conference calling for small businesses. Sign up and receive your own free conference call number and directions for use.

Women's Business Centers—Assistance at ninety-three centers in forty-six states and four territories: *www.sba.gov/womeninbusiness/wbcs.html*

Women's Network for Entrepreneurial Training—Mentoring by successful businesswomen at more than 160 roundtable groups nationwide: *www.sba.gov/womeninbusiness/wnet.html*

"Your Business Today" radio program—Provides daily news, handy tips, and resources for small business owners: *www.YourBusinessToday.com*

Women VCs

ABS Capital Partners
Laura Witt, principal
One South Street, 25th Floor
Baltimore, MD 21202-3220
Phone: 410-895-4400
Fax: 410-895-4380
lwitt@abscapital.com

Blue Water Capital
Kathleen Millier, Associate
1420 Beverly Road
Suite 300
McLean, VA 22101
Phone: 703-790-8821
Fax: 703-448-1849
millier@bluewatercapital.com

Draper International
Robin Richards Donohoe
Managing Director
50 California, Suite 2925
San Francisco, CA 94111
Phone: 415-616-4050
Fax: 415-616-4060
www.draperrichards.com

MCI Worldcom Venture Fund
Susan Mayer, President
1801 Pennsylvania Avenue, NW
Washington, DC 20006
Phone: 202-887-2299
Fax: 202-887-3226
susan.mayer@wcom.com

Smith Whiley & Company
General Partner
SW Pelham Fund and the Bon Secours Community Investment
Fund
242 Trumbull Street
Hartford, CT 06103
Phone: 860-548-2513
Invests in women and minority-owned businesses.

Women's Growth Capital Fund
Patty Abramson, Managing Director
1054 31st Street, NW, Suite 110
Washington, DC 20007
Phone: 202-342-1431
Fax: 202-342-1203
patty@wgcf.com

Angel Networks

Garage.com
Yazam.com

Venture Capitalists

www.startups.com
www.vcapital.com
www.venturelist.com
www.vfinance.com

Business Plan Consultants (people who write business plans)

www.growthink.com

Books

The E Myth: Why Most Small Businesses Don't Work and What to Do About It by Michael Gerber (Harper Business, April 1995)

The Fundamentals of Venture Capital by Joseph Bartlett (Madison Books, August 1999)

Money Rules: Personal Finance in Your 20s and 30s by Juliette Fairley; see Chapter 17. (Prentice Hall Press, 2001)

....

CHAPTER 9

Money, Men, and Love

Competition for Men in the Cities

A major drawback of living in cities is that single women face more competition from other women. American women outnumber men by nearly 8 million, according to the U.S. Census Bureau, which means that we'd better not be banking on a husband.

We need to get a profession and a job in case we don't wind up married.

If you are in the dating game and seriously man-hunting, this chapter gives tips on how to handle cash and love. If you don't need advice about finding a man, then skip this chapter because it contains a *frank* discussion about the reality of money as it pertains to love relationships.

As a result of the competition for a mate, women are more inclined to want to look their best and spend money they don't have on clothes, shoes, and hair in the hopes of attracting a refined caveman.

In addition to looking their best, women have to get an edge somehow over the competition. You can do that by wearing an interesting T-shirt, walking a cute dog, or donning a colorful hat, original scarf, or neckpiece.

"You have to look at your social routine and decide whether you are going to the places that are best for you. If so, you may want to take it one step further and get involved by joining an organization and doing volunteer work," says Robin Gorman Newman, founder of *www.LoveCoach.com*, a website for singles. "Make yourself part of something so you are really getting to know people. It's easier to get noticed that way."

Don't Be a Drain

When you have a cutie on the line, let him pay on the first date. But it's always classy to offer to pay. By the third date, if you like the guy, you may want to have a conversation about money. Find out how he has handled money in past dating relationships. Does he expect you to pay at some point? Does he want you to pay your share? You may want to be courted but don't be a drain. Reciprocate by buying dessert somewhere else, picking up the movie tickets, getting play tickets, or cooking him dinner some other time. But it shouldn't be a scorecard situation. Men may wonder if you are going out on a date for a free meal. By offering to pay, you're making it clear that you are there because you want to be with that person. It goes a long way in building a partnership relationship.

Most people don't enter a relationship talking about money. We talk about dating, we talk about other people's relationships, we talk about our careers, but we don't talk about money. Once it's established that you are a couple, talk about your long-term financial goals.

"If one person is going to the racetrack while the other person is saving to buy a house in two years, that is going to be a problem," says Jennifer Openshaw, founder of the Women's Financial Network.

Women Who Are Good with Money

Many single women fending for themselves have sharpened their money skills to the point of being very good with their money.

A man who admires your money skills can be one of two things: a good guy who is appreciative of modern times or a man on the make. Trust your gut to figure out which one he is. Men who are intimidated by money-savvy women may have grown up with a mother who took the check from the father in a domineering way and may fear being controlled. Otherwise, the man's a loser.

"Forget the background. If looking at facts and figures makes a guy insecure, I'd have real doubts from the gal's point of view as to what is going on here," Peter Calfee said.

How to Be Financially Astute in a Love Relationship

The stereotype of young single women is that they like dresses, jewelry, money, and things that are consumable. The perception is that women don't really understand financial matters. Prove them wrong by educating yourself about finances. Most men would be positive and responsive to a woman who demonstrated that she can handle money, stick to a budget, have extra cash left over, and not be frivolous. A woman can show her astuteness by being upfront with what she needs.

Financial astuteness also means not giving a man access to your credit card or cosigning for a loan. (More on this later.)

Dealing with a Man's Money Flaws

No man is perfect on the inside, even if he looks perfect on the outside. Inevitably, you'll get to know your new man and find that he is either a tightwad or a spendthrift.

What you have to do is recognize his financial flaw and figure out how you can neutralize or massage those financial faults without him finding out about it.

If he is a spendthrift, he may think that he can go out and make money whenever he needs it. As his mate, create a financial goal, such as retirement, and convince him to contribute money to it every month.

But instead of asking that he contribute $500 monthly, you may want to double it to $1,000 so that you wind up with $12,000 stashed away at the end of the year instead of $6,000.

That is the gentle, delicate, loving way that you can handle a spendthrift.

Dealing with a tightwad is a bit more difficult. You may want to find another boyfriend.

Your Lover's Financial Past

Your lover's financial problems can affect your future in many ways, including not qualifying for a low-interest-rate loan when buying a home.

If he took out student loans and didn't pay them off or declared bankruptcy, you could end up paying a much higher interest rate than with a man who had been responsible with past debt.

Check on your man's financial past just like you check on his family history or career history.

It may sound outrageous, but you may want to ask for his credit report at the altar, because when marrying, you're merging your finances, and his past habits can have a financial impact on your current and future financial well-being. Remember, though, that if you ask for his credit report, be prepared to turn yours over as well.

The first time you visit his apartment, look around. A person's environment reveals a lot. What is he spending his money on? Does he have a flashy car and no furniture? If he has no furniture, is he paying off student loans and trying to start saving for his first home? These are things that you can ask upfront.

While you're at it, run a civil and criminal check throughout the databases of the state!

Love and Credit

It's important to discuss your potential spouse's credit past because after marriage you could be responsible for debts that were incurred by him prior to marriage.

Past due debts, back child support that's due, or liens (legal claims) against him don't mean you have to break up with him. Just make sure they are settled *before* you get married.

"If he has back taxes, claim Injured Spouse and you may not be held liable for that individual's tax debt prior to the marriage," says Roland J. Chupik, president and CEO of Consumer Credit Counseling Service of Greater San Antonio.

Single women need to be practical. Keep your eyes open. Oftentimes, single women get taken advantage of by good-looking men.

All that glitters may not be gold. Watch your back!

....

Example

Cindy Lee fell in love with a tall blond Russian man who had big dreams of starting a business. Cindy had a great job as a CFO at a major accounting firm in Washington, D.C., while her boyfriend had been floundering for years as a would-be entrepreneur.

Thirty-year-old Cindy didn't pay attention when her boyfriend told her that he was in debt for $10,000 in student loans. The slight Asian woman was so taken with her Viking-looking boyfriend that she cosigned a loan for her man.

His business did well for a year, but when the market dropped and sales fizzled out, he asked Cindy to cosign another loan to keep the company afloat.

After the second year, the business closed down. Cindy came home one day to an empty apartment. The blond Russian had taken their furniture and disappeared while she was at work. Cindy was left with $16,000 in loans that she had to pay back because the handsome Slav had returned to Moscow.

"I could kick myself," Cindy said. "I really believed that he loved me and that we would be successful together. I never dreamed he would stick me with the bill. It's been really painful, emotionally and financially."

....

Rules for Living Together

When women fall in love, they're more likely to give up their apartments and move in with the guy, but that may be a big mistake if the couple breaks up.

A better solution would be to hold on to your apartment by getting a roommate who helps pay the rent or by continuing to pay rent for your apartment and using it as a crash pad whenever you feel claustrophobic at your boyfriend's apartment.

Be smart. The old attitude of "If I'm worth it, let's see the ring" still stands in the new millennium. Keep your apartment and continue paying rent while loverboy pays the rent for his apartment, which you both live in.

Who you are and what you have is worth a lot. So tell him, "I'm not going to just toss that out the window and bop into your life for you to have me dumped on a doorstep somewhere when you get tired."

"That's the downside of guys. Often, they are users and takers. That goes back to the primal aspect of the Stone Age structure," says Peter Calfee.

Another tendency is to commingle your checking accounts and benefits. Don't do it. Keep everything separate so that you can break away easily without conflict about who owns what.

For example, if the rent is $1,000 and your share is $400, you would simply write a check for $400 to your beau so that he could pay the rent out of his checkbook.

We women tend to get caught up in the emotions of a relationship, the excitement of a potential marriage, and forget that we need to take care of our own financial security.

When moving in with a man, it's a good idea to ask your respective attorneys to draw up a cohabitation agreement.

To protect yourself, the agreement should cover what happens to the property upon termination of the relationship, what is your obligation to contribute to the support of the household during the relationship, and what is your obligation to pay financial support in the event the relationship dissolves.

If there were two residences—for example, a house in the country and an apartment in the city—you would want to make sure that they are included in the agreement.

"The agreement puts everything into context and makes sure that you've covered all your bases," says Arlene Dubin, a partner and lawyer with RubinBaum, a law firm in Manhattan.

Joint Tenancy

Putting your property in joint tenancy with right of survivorship means that each of the parties in a relationship has a right to the home. So, if the relationship breaks up, there is the mutual intent that each of you would be entitled to half of it.

"You may have to sell it and split it up, but at least you are going to be entitled to half of it. You are not going to just leave after a long-term relationship and end up with not even enough money to find another residence. And the right of survivorship is what would give you the house in the event of death," says Dubin.

Go to an attorney to establish joint tenancy with right of survivorship.

Common Law

Common law marriage exists in eleven states and the District of Columbia.

To benefit from a common law marriage, you have to prove that the two of you agreed, either in writing or orally, that you are husband and wife. And you must have acquired a reputation as a married couple. For example, when you registered in a hotel, you checked in as Mr. and Mrs., or people in the neighborhood know you as husband and wife.

You plan to fail when you fail to plan. Chapter 10 will help you devise a financial backup plan in case plan A with Mr. Right falls through.

Resources

Prenups for Lovers: A Romantic Guide to Prenuptial Agreements by
    Arlene Dubin (Villard Books, February 2001)

www.match.com

www.hurrydate.com

CHAPTER 10

••

Plan B for Backup Money

Metropolitan maidens often face crisis situations that rural women driving pickup trucks never even think about. For example, when the handsome investment banker you meet at the dry cleaners' invites you to his firm's annual dinner at the United Nations, what do you wear? Or when you're next in line on the waiting list for a $4,000 hard Hermès Birkin bag, where do you get the benjamins?

Most financial planners will tell you to save enough cash to cover three to six months of living expenses—such as rent, food, and utilities—in case you lose your job or are unexpectedly hit with a large bill. We city girls need a prudent reserve to cover surprise expenses, such as a new designer dress for a once-in-a-lifetime date with a hot celebrity.

Some city girls don't acknowledge the need for emergency funds because of the easy access to credit cards. You may say, "Why do I need savings when I have a credit card?" The answer lies within the question. You want a stash of cash so that you won't have to use that credit card because you pay a high price for financing a surprise expense with a credit card. Try 20-percent interest, in some cases! Credit cards create a vicious cycle of more debt and little savings. (More on debt in Chapter 11.)

•••

Example

Caitlin Bailey proudly cut up her credit cards in January. She thought she was on the right track by operating on a cash basis until her trusty hand-me-down Mercedes broke down in March. The flame-haired news assistant didn't anticipate car repairs in her budget and had no access to an emergency expense fund. The twenty-four-year-old had to ride the bus system in Las Vegas and rely on favors from friends until her next paycheck ten days later.

"I almost broke down and got a credit card. But I had gone a year without credit cards and didn't want to start the habit again. So I just rolled with the punches. It was tough for those ten days but I got through it," Caitlin said.

If she'd built an emergency expense fund, Caitlin would have had the $1,500 necessary to pay for the car repairs in cash. The lipstick-lean info-babe has learned a lesson.

"I've started putting away $100 a month for emergencies. I have about $900 in my savings account, and I still haven't used a credit card! Maybe in a couple of years I'll have enough money to buy a new car in cash," she said.

....

You'll feel your self-esteem rise as the dollars add up in your savings account. There's nothing like knowing you have money in the bank. It beats the security of a size 2 dress any day.

Stashing away enough money to cover three to six months' living expenses can seem a bit daunting, to say the least. Don't let the task deter you.

Start small. Instead of having a goal of saving three months' expenses, aim to gather only one month's expenses. Once you have a month under your belt, you can increase your contributions incrementally over time. Before you know it, you'll have two months and then three months of living expenses tucked away. It's easier to save when your income is rising. (Read Chapter 7 on careers.)

Once you've saved the money, don't lock it up in illiquid investments. Instead of stockpiling cash in a certificate of deposit (CD), put the money in a savings account or money market mutual fund. The interest rate on money market mutual funds can be 2 to 3 percent higher than a bank savings account. The downside is that money market funds are not federally insured whereas banks usually are. The problem with CDs is that you'll forfeit any interest earned if you withdraw the money early. One good investment strategy is to invest in an S&P 500 index fund, such as Vanguard or Schwab 1000.

It's important to get started saving and investing while you're in your twenties and thirties because of the power of compounding. Compounding is when money accrues because of the rate of return. The higher the rate of return, the more money compounds. The younger you are when you start putting away money, the more money you accumulate over time.

If you put away $2,000 a month at thirty years old at a 6 percent annual rate of return, you'd have $77,985 after twenty years. But if you had started five years earlier, when you were twenty-five years old, you'd have $116,312 after twenty-five years. You can see the loss that waiting five years creates.

Another example is the case of two twin sisters in Exhibit 10.1. Jill (left column) starts saving $2,000 a month at the age of nineteen and stops at twenty-six while Judy (right column) doesn't start saving until twenty-seven but continues until she is sixty-five years old. At sixty-five, Jill will have $2.2 million while Judy only has $1.5 million.

One way to take advantage of compounding is to dollar cost average, which means putting away a set amount of money into a mutual fund account or IRA account on a monthly basis. The best way to dollar cost average is to take advantage of payroll deduction. If you authorize your mutual fund company to withdraw $100

How To Research Mutual Funds

1. Pick a mutual fund.

2. Note its market symbol.

3. Go to *morningstar.com*.

4. Enter the fund's symbol.

5. Compare performance numbers for the year to date, one year, and five year.

6. Look for consistent performance and numbers rather than one outstanding year.

7. Make a note of the fund's manager. Does he or she have a track record?

8. Examine fees and the fund's operating expenses.

9. Consider whether the fund charges a sales commission or load on your purchase.

---

automatically every month from your checking account, you'll never miss the money.

The rate of return on the money invested or saved doesn't have a dramatic effect on the end result until the account begins to amass, which is usually about eight to twelve years later. At that point, it flip-flops and the rate of return matters more than the contribution.

To figure out how many years it will take for your money to double, use the Rule of 72. Take the interest rate you are earning and divide it into 72. For example, with 5 percent interest (72 divided by 5), in 14.4 years your money will double. With 10 percent interest, your money doubles in 7.2 years.

Why Invest Early?

Year	Age	Annual Savings	Amount Accumulated	Age	Annual Savings	Amount Accumulated
1	19	$ 2,000	$ 2,240	19		$
2	20	$ 2,000	$ 4,479	20		$
3	21	$ 2,000	$ 7,559	21		$
4	22	$ 2,000	$ 10,706	22		$
5	23	$ 2,000	$ 14,230	23		$
6	24	$ 2,000	$ 18,178	24		$
7	25	$ 2,000	$ 22,599	25		$
8	26	$ 2,000	$ 27,551	26		$
9	27		$ 30,857	27	$ 2,000	$ 2,240
10	28		$ 34,560	28	$ 2,000	$ 4,479
11	29		$ 38,708	29	$ 2,000	$ 7,559
12	30		$ 43,353	30	$ 2,000	$ 10,706
13	31		$ 48,555	31	$ 2,000	$ 14,230
14	32		$ 54,381	32	$ 2,000	$ 18,178
15	33		$ 60,907	33	$ 2,000	$ 22,599
16	34		$ 68,216	34	$ 2,000	$ 27,551
17	35		$ 76,402	35	$ 2,000	$ 33,097
18	36		$ 85,570	36	$ 2,000	$ 39,309
19	37		$ 95,839	37	$ 2,000	$ 46,266
20	38		$ 107,339	38	$ 2,000	$ 54,058
21	39		$ 120,222	39	$ 2,000	$ 62,785
22	40		$ 134,646	40	$ 2,000	$ 72,559
23	41		$ 150,804	41	$ 2,000	$ 83,507
24	42		$ 168,900	42	$ 2,000	$ 95,767
25	43		$ 189,168	43	$ 2,000	$ 109,499
26	44		$ 211,869	44	$ 2,000	$ 124,879
27	45		$ 237,293	45	$ 2,000	$ 142,105
28	46		$ 265,768	46	$ 2,000	$ 161,397
29	47		$ 297,660	47	$ 2,000	$ 183,005
30	48		$ 333,379	48	$ 2,000	$ 207,206
31	49		$ 373,385	49	$ 2,000	$ 234,310
32	50		$ 418,191	50	$ 2,000	$ 264,668
33	51		$ 468,374	51	$ 2,000	$ 298,668
34	52		$ 524,579	52	$ 2,000	$ 336,748
35	53		$ 587,528	53	$ 2,000	$ 379,398
36	54		$ 658,032	54	$ 2,000	$ 427,166
37	55		$ 736,996	55	$ 2,000	$ 480,665
38	56		$ 825,435	56	$ 2,000	$ 540,585
39	57		$ 924,487	57	$ 2,000	$ 607,695
40	58		$ 1,035,426	58	$ 2,000	$ 682,859
41	59		$ 1,159,677	59	$ 2,000	$ 767,042
42	60		$ 1,298,838	60	$ 2,000	$ 861,327
43	61		$ 1,454,699	61	$ 2,000	$ 966,926
44	62		$ 1,629,263	62	$ 2,000	$ 1,085,197
45	63		$ 1,824,774	63	$ 2,000	$ 1,217,661
46	64		$ 2,043,747	64	$ 2,000	$ 1,366,020
47	65		$	65	$ 2,000	$ 1,532,183

		$ 16,000		Total Amount Invested	$ 78,000
Ending Value at Age 65		$ 2,288,997		Ending Value at Age 65	$ 1,532,183
Jill				Judy	

Assuming 12% annual rate of return
Assuming $2,000 IRA Contribution made on January 2nd annually.

Save early and save whenever possible. Put as much as you can into tax-deferred vehicles, such as 401(k) plans and IRAs.

Some of you may wonder where you will get the money to begin investing. Here are some savings tips to help you uncover spare cash:

- Find a checking account that pays interest but beware of high monthly fees.
- Put your income tax refund directly into savings along with any other sudden windfalls.
- Get a side or freelance job and put that income toward investments.
- Rather than having $100 deposited directly into your savings account, arrange to have $30 a week deducted for savings.
- When you're tempted to buy something frivolous, think in terms of how many work hours it would require to pay for it. For example, a $500 pair of diamond earrings would cost you 164 hours of work if you make $30 an hour.

Situations in Which Single Urban Woman May Need Backup Money

- Finding a steal of an apartment, which requires a hefty security deposit
- Down payment for a home
- Car repairs
- Man-hunting vacation to Club Med with girlfriends
- 70 percent off–year-end sale on designer dresses and purses at your local department store
- Half-price-off gym membership promotion

- Once-in-a-lifetime opportunity to go on a ski trip to Aspen with potential hot husband, which requires you to buy cute ski outfits

- Winter blues requiring a quick getaway to the Caribbean or Hawaii

- Registering for that infamous $500 screenwriting class you've been dying to sign up for

- A facelift for your fiftieth birthday five to ten years from now

- A week-long spa retreat in Santa Fe, New Mexico, after teary breakup with "Mr. Right"

- Golf camp and tennis lessons

- Starting your own business

- Decorating your home

- A fur coat for your first opening night gala or movie premiere

- Louis Vuitton carry-on luggage so that you can travel in style

- Sundance Film Festival or Cannes Film Festival

- The French Riviera in August

- Continuing education courses at local university or Learning Annex

- State-of-the-art computer for online dating

Now that you know how to build up a prudent reserve so that you won't have to use credit cards, Chapter 11 will teach those who are already in debt how to get out.

CHAPTER 11

....

Plastic Can Be Drastic

Why City Women Are More Susceptible to Debt

Although cities offer endless cultural and social offerings, these activities require money.

As a result, city women may have perfectly manicured fingertips, engagement-filled agendas, and hipper-than-thou weekend affairs, but they also tend to incur debt to keep up appearances.

It's not so easy to resist constant retail assaults while walking down the street on the way home from work, especially when credit card companies are so eagerly willing to increase the credit limits of professional city women.

Complicating matters is that women in their twenties and thirties have many starting-out expenses, such as their first professional wardrobe, the first sofa, their first apartment, and many other hidden costs. In addition, we live in a consumer society, where young people are encouraged to spend their money.

Life in the big cities is more expensive than in rural areas. As a result, single women tend to finance a greater portion of their lifestyle on credit. Additionally, women are more likely to have a lower annual income than men at the same age and position while having to spend more to maintain their appearance. Women's clothing, dry cleaning, hair styling, manicures, waxing, and grooming products are more expensive than men's.

Credit spending is greater in larger cities because options—and subsequently credit lines themselves—are heftier than those in smaller towns. And what can we blame for these unfair, inhuman temptations? "Marketing," explains Roland J. Chupik, president and CEO of Consumer Credit Counseling Service of Greater San Antonio, "says you can have it and that you can get it immediately if you use credit."

City women aren't necessarily careless or vulnerable with their money; they are simply living the lifestyle that surrounds them. Urban amenities such as the Friday-night theater outing, unavoidably expensive housing, and the innocent lunch-break shopping trip are all part of what makes city spending never ending. Young women get sucked into buying, buying, and more buying when they are least capable of paying. Bringing home lower wages than their male counterparts and pressure from friends to spend combine to create a dangerous recipe for debt. "They go out and buy this and that and just follow the leader," says Lawrence Novick, a stockbroker. "It could be just a herd mentality."

How Debt Affects Your Future Wealth

When you get into debt, you're mortgaging your future income. If you're spending today on a credit card, tomorrow's work day will pay for the purchase.

If you're using tomorrow's dollar to pay for it today, then you can't use tomorrow's dollars to save for future wealth. Being in perpetual credit card debt prevents you from saving for retirement and other life goals.

••

Example

Taylor Selaward, a Los Angeles publicist, is like many thirty-year-old single women. She enjoys an occasional trip abroad and designer shoes. But eight years after graduating from college, Taylor is still struggling to make ends meet. She owes a total of $66,000 in a car note, student loans, and credit card repayments to such companies as Visa, Discover, Victoria's Secret, and Lord & Taylor.

She pays $1,500 a month toward debt repayment and often feels stressed by her financial limitations.

"I feel stress when I want to go on a fabulous vacation to France or Italy and I can't because I have debt obligations. Or if I want that $500 pair of Gucci shoes and that $300 BCBG dress and I know I can't get them, then I'm stressed," she says.

Her debt history began immediately after college when she was unable to pay off her student loans. She bought a Toyota 4Runner last year, which added to her already existing debt burden.

Her fear is that she'll meet Mr. Right and be forced to air her dirty "debt" laundry to the man. "If a man can love you through debt, I believe anything's possible," she says.

The blonde bombshell is not beyond dreaming that Oprah will pay off her debts in one of her "Wildest Dreams" shows or praying for a big Hollywood deal.

"It would be beyond my wildest dream," says Taylor. "Then my future husband wouldn't know!"

In the meantime, she tries to use cash as often as possible because she knows that is the secret to debt reduction and has set her sights on an aggressive short-term goal. "I'm definitely trying to be at a zero balance one day soon."

....

Debt Pitfalls

The debt habit of women in their twenties and thirties often has its roots in college.

As college students, we're often intoxicated by our newly acquired independence and tend to overindulge and overspend with inaugural credit cards that have enticingly low monthly pay-ments and interest rates. Eventually, careless spending snowballs and lingers stubbornly after graduation, like that pesky C- in bio lab sophomore year.

"Typically what we see," says Chupik, "is a college student who starts out with one card and then the limit will go up and then she will get another card. And before you know it, she's got five cards and they've all got $5,000 balances on them and the person is $25,000 in debt."

Not a pretty picture for a twenty-two-year-old woman already saddled with student loans and the daunting task of entering an unforgiving job market.

The long-term effects of relying on plastic can be drastic, to say the least.

Six Questions to Determine If You Are in or Headed for Financial Trouble

1. Are you unsure about how much you owe? Do you skip some bills to pay others?

2. Do you have insufficient cash saved to see you through an emergency?

3. If you lost your job, would you have trouble paying for your basic living expenses?

4. Are you receiving calls from creditors about overdue bills?

5. Are you using an increasing percentage of your monthly income to pay off debts?

6. Can you make only the minimum payments on your credit cards?

If you answered yes to

1–2 questions: You may be developing financial problems. Consider visiting a budget counselor to avoid the risk of serious trouble in the future.

3–5 questions: You are on the edge of financial disaster. Get started today to develop a plan to regain control of your situation.

6 questions: You are in over your head. Act now to take control of your finances. Use a budget counselor to develop a realistic plan to repay debt.

Source: National Foundation for Credit Counseling (NFCC)

••

Example of Woman in Debt: Maureen Quinn

Los Angeles native Maureen Quinn is an ambitious recruiter for a temporary employment placement agency. She makes about $32,000 a year plus commissions, but has $15,000 in debt from credit card spending in college. In order to pay back her debts faster, Maureen swallowed her pride, put her social life on the back burner, and made a drastic decision: She moved back in with Mom and Dad.

"I'd like to be paid off in eighteen months, but I have to forfeit 50 percent of my paycheck in order to do that, which means I have to live at home."

Her debt problem began in college after "low-interest" credit card marketing geared toward students got the better of her. "They have brochures for credit cards tucked in every single book that you buy from the campus bookstore," she says. "They are plastered everywhere." Despite not having an income during school, she started buying clothes, going out, partying, and living beyond her means.

"It was very easy to access credit cards; I just started spending," she said.

Today, nearly two years out of school, Maureen makes monthly payments to Citibank, Discover, MBNA, and retail companies such as Macy's and The Limited/Express.

During her time of debt repayment, the twenty-four-year-old has had to table travel plans, recreational spending, and the clothing sprees that got her into trouble in the first place.

"It's really stressful. It holds me back from doing other things I would have done, like travel, move out, have extra income to do things that my peers are doing," she said.

As Maureen continues to live the life of debt repayment "one card at a time," she reflects on her college days through a lens of regret. Is her careless spending in college a major hindrance to making ends meet today? Was it a big mistake?

Her answer: "Definitely."

. . . .

A major fault among credit-addicted female students is their lack of expense analysis. What exactly *are* they buying? Well, the usual suspects are there—clothing, purses, cosmetics—along with a whole new brand of college-specific necessities: books, fast food, and alcohol. Many of these "expenses" are nothing but assaults on their future credit histories.

"If they had to pay cash for those things," says Marion Loftus, the director of Consumer Credit Counseling Services (CCCS) in Pittsburgh, "or even write a check for them, in many cases they probably wouldn't buy. But putting it on a card makes it feel like you are not really spending the money."

These habits usually do not cease upon graduating. In fact, they likely worsen as young, single women migrate to urban areas where they compensate for being underpaid by being overdressed. The secret to stay out of that dark, despairing, hopeless debt hole is to ask yourself: Would I buy this item if I only had cash?

How Debt Catches Up with You

Like the powers that be at a monthly music club, creditors always find you. The difference is that with debt, the consequences are much more dire than the nuisance of mailing back an unwanted CD. For many women, overextending their financial means becomes as dangerous as a mind-altering drug. Credit spending is addictive.

The formula for imminent financial disaster is a basic one: Charging more than you have the ability to pay equals debt. If you can only afford $50 a month toward your debt, but you have charged to the point where your payments are $100, this will catch up with you.

For example, a $60 minimum payment on a $3,000 credit card balance with an interest rate of 18 percent would take nearly eight years to pay off and cost a person a whopping $2,586 in interest. By paying an additional $30 a month, the debt would be paid off in half the time and with almost $1,200 in interest charges to spare. Study Table 11.1 to get clear on the long-term financial damage.

Table 11.1

The Cost of Debt

Interest you'll pay on a $10,000 debt over three years:

RATE	AMOUNT
6.0%	$952
9.9%	$1,599
21.9%	$3,730

Like alcoholism, extending credit lines to buy the things that "make you happy" becomes a drug of choice, a way to feel good.

But it doesn't happen overnight, which is why it catches women off guard years later. The debt spiral starts out slow and easy with "low" monthly payments and "small" balances. But after months of gradual accumulation, debt seems to strike when least expected —or wanted. Frantic consumers often take cash advances from credit cards—and sign up for new ones—to pay for important life items like groceries and gasoline, at which point the concept of spiraling out of control is a way of life that can be maintained only with more debt.

Once caught in that cycle, it's very hard to get out.

Even the most well-intended repayment schedule won't erase years of accumulation unless you stop incurring any new debt. Making minimum payments on a credit card can last for twenty years because your minimum payment is only going toward interest on the principal.

Do yourself a favor: Buy a paper shredder from K-Mart, and whenever you get one of those tempting "reward" letters sent by computer saying "Hi! You've been so great we are increasing your limit by another $1,500," shred it, and call the credit card company to cancel the account. But you may have to call twice because they often "conveniently" omit your first request to cancel.

Bad Credit/Credit Reports

After you have accepted your bad credit standing (which is the first step to recovery!), the best thing to do is obtain a copy of your credit report. If you are past due with creditors, either through a consumer credit counseling agency or on your own, make some payments if possible and see if you can get the creditor to bring your standing up to date. Even the lowest, on-time payments will allow you to establish a more current history of better credit.

The easiest way to receive a copy of your credit report is to contact credit bureaus.

It is not good enough to obtain a copy of just one of your credit reports. To really monitor your credit history, obtain a copy from all three major credit-reporting bureaus. Here are their phone numbers:

Equifax: 1-800-685-1111

Experian (formerly TRW): 1-888-397-3742

Trans Union: 1-800-916-8800

There is a free—but possibly embarrassing—way to get a copy of your credit report. When you apply for a credit card at a retail store, for example, and you are denied, you are then entitled to a free credit report. In what's called a Letter of Denial, the store is obligated to provide you with the name of the reporting repository or agency from which it pulled your information. Then you can receive a copy of your report from that company. You also can visit *www.creditreports.com* on the Web, which allows you to order a credit report online.

Maintaining a current appraisal of your credit history should be an annual—if not year-long—activity. Review the credit report religiously for irregularities, because if there is a problem, such as an incorrect charge or balance, writing letters to get it repaired can be a long, painful process.

Like our souls, credit reports are eternal; from the time you begin using credit to the day you die. Your credit history is a lifelong activity and who's to say your debts won't follow you into your next life! Better to pay them off now than carry over debts.

How to Get Out of Debt

The fastest way to get out of debt is to commit to increasing those minimum payments. Double, triple, or quadruple the minimum payment! When you're done with one card, move on to the next one. Pay off the cards with the highest interest rates first, and if you inherit a lump sum, or get birthday money, consider dumping a portion on debt repayment. The idea is to get out of debt as fast as you can and start operating on a cash basis.

Seven Steps to Getting Out of Debt

Step 1. Stop incurring more debt—unless it's an emergency.

Step 2. Evaluate your financial condition. Stop being vague. Calculate how much you owe. Take a close look at every creditor you owe, understand exactly how much it's costing you to have each particular debt, and review your payment history with all your creditors.

Step 3. Pay on time—no matter what it takes! You'll avoid late fees, which do add up.

Step 4. Create a budget and stick to it.

Step 5.   Put as much money toward debt repayment as you possibly can without neglecting your self-care.

Step 6.   Pay off the smallest balance or pay off the highest interest rate debt first.

Step 7.   Try to live solvently, without debt.

Many credit experts say that paying off the balance with highest interest rate makes sense, but Roland Chupik disagrees. "If you are paying off a higher balance, it's going to take you longer to pay it off. It's true you're going to save some interest, but psychologically you're not going to have that feeling of accomplishment that you will have if you pay off the smallest balance first," he says. Paying off the smaller balance makes you feel better about your progress and also frees up more money to put toward the next highest balance. Whatever strategy you settle on, just start paying off your debt!

Borrowing more money to pay off existing debt can be dangerous when you consolidate debt but don't close the lines of credit that you just consolidated, and continue to use them. You'll accrue an even greater debt with multiple lines of credit open, which, if used, will only dig you a deeper hole into debt.

A safe but slower way is to create a budget, cut out unnecessary expenses, and put as much money as you can toward paying off that debt. It may take a while, but if you add just $10 more to your payment each month, a balance of $2,000 at 18 percent doesn't have to take twenty years to pay off.

Creating a budget doesn't mean simply jotting down how much you spend on rent, groceries, and the light bill. It involves tracking your expenses for at least three months. Carry a little notebook with you every day and write down every expenditure you make, right down to chewing gum from the newspaper stand. At the end of the month, you will see exactly where your money is going. (More on this in Chapter 12.)

For women in serious debt, their expenses are typically higher than their incomes. So the first thing that must take place in balancing your budget is deciding what is a "need" and what is a "want." Needs have to come first. Women also have a way of saying things like cell phones are "needs" for the safety issue, or cable is a "need" because they can't get anything else on TV.

If you're running from the law, if you're not answering your phone because the creditors are hounding you, or if you're suicidal over your debt situation, you probably need to go to a nonprofit credit counseling agency for other options. Selling valuables, like Grandma's prized wedding ring, should really be a last resort. It is only a short-term solution to a more serious problem, and later you may regret having hocked an heirloom.

Nonprofit versus For-Profit Credit Counseling Agencies

The main difference between nonprofit and for-profit credit counseling agencies is not so much about the type of service as it is the fees they charge. Nonprofit agency fees tend to be free or charge very low fees. For-profits will charge higher amounts because their funding sources are more limited.

Consumers can go to a nonprofit organization to ask questions, get help drawing up a household budget, or find out about a variety of programs and resources—from online chats, self-help publications, and community seminars to long-term debt management programs.

"If it looks like someone is drowning in debt and it would take years and years to get out of it, we toss them a life preserver and put them on a debt management plan," says Howard Dvorkin, president of Consolidated Credit Counseling Services in Fort Lauderdale, a nonprofit credit counseling agency.

A for-profit firm usually negotiates settlements with creditors for people who are on the brink of bankruptcy, who have mostly collateralized debts, or who are being sued. Many people who get turned down by a nonprofit agency may turn to a for-profit center because they can't meet the minimum payment requirements of a debt management plan.

Often for-profit companies work on contingency fees. They can cost customers 10 cents to 60 cents for every $1 of debt, depending on the customer's ability to repay. The advantage to the client is avoiding bankruptcy.

The disadvantages: The person may have to tap a valuable asset, such as retirement savings, and a quick fix might not change bad habits like a long-term payoff plan would.

The advantages of using a nonprofit organization are that it can reduce or eliminate interest charges on credit cards and unsecured loans, it may be able to reduce your payments up to 50 percent, and it can end harassing creditor phone calls. Find a list of non-profits at the National Foundation for Credit Counseling website, *www.NFCC.org*, or look in the yellow pages under credit counseling in your city and then call to find out if they are nonprofit.

Six Bankruptcy Prevention Tips

1. *Develop spending plans.* Have both long-term and short-term spending plans that include fixed, variable, and periodic expenses. Your budget should include fixed expenses, like mortgage and monthly premiums, as well as variable expenses, such as utilities and entertainment. Resolve to plan ahead for periodic expenses such as car repairs, vacations, holiday spending, taxes, and home repairs.

2. *Reduce your debt.* Make a commitment to reduce your overall debt. Pay more than the minimum balance on outstanding credit balances. Delay unnecessary expenditures until your current bills are paid.

3. *Build your assets.* Savings can help carry you through emergency situations like a temporary layoff. You should build up to three to six months of living expenses in savings. Once you have done so, keep saving and investing for expenses and retirement.

4. *Insure your future.* Get disability insurance. If you rent your home, make sure you have adequate coverage for your personal belongings in case of theft or fire.

5. *Use credit wisely.* Limit yourself to one or two credit cards. Use the cards with the lowest rates and pay off your balance each month. Carefully review each month's expenses to see if you are overspending in a certain area; then adjust your spending to keep credit balances from creeping up.

> **6.** *Get help early.* Before filing for bankruptcy, make sure you have researched all the options available. If you realize that you are having financial trouble or would like help setting financial priorities, seek counseling help. The 1,400 member offices of National Foundation for Credit Counseling offer free or low-cost financial education workshops, budgeting assistance, and credit counseling to consumers nationwide.
>
> *Source:* National Foundation for Credit Counseling

Pros and Cons of Consolidation

If you borrow $10,000 from a bank to repay your debt, depending on your credit history, most banks can get a rate at 11 percent. Most credit card rates are between 15 and 21 percent, so you can substantially reduce the interest rate by borrowing from a bank.

Pros

1. Enjoy lower interest rates in repaying credit debt.

2. Only make one payment.

3. Establish another line of credit.

Cons

1. You've got lines of credit that are still open. The tendency is to use the line of credit that is now available, which gets you deeper in debt.

2. Continuing to use cards while repaying, which results in more debt.

3. Getting consolidation loans from finance companies instead of banks and finding out that finance company rates are substantially higher.

4. Falling prey to teaser rates, where the rate is 3 or 6 percent for six months, after which time the rate goes up. Many women fail to see how high the rate will climb, and if they have a lot of debt, they may not qualify to get another credit card with a lower interest rate. When teasers expire, many people get another "teaser rate" and put everything on that card. Instead of getting out of debt, they are increasing it.

Debt Repair Agencies

The only sure and solid way to repair a credit history is by paying bills when they are due and making sure your credit report contains correct information.

Not all debt repair agencies are scams, but be careful. You don't want to spend money on a debt repair agency that you could have put toward repayment. Try to do your own credit repair before resorting to an agency. If you find an error on your credit report, contact the credit reporting bureaus.

If you don't have time to do your own credit repair, before hiring a debt repair agency, check out the firm with the Better Business Bureau to make sure it is legitimate.

There is no legal way to change a delinquent payment history, except if there was an error.

There are a lot of cons to these agencies. They charge very high fees—sometimes $500 to $1,000—to do the kind of service that an individual can do. They can remove errors, but they don't tell you how long they can have it removed.

Remember this: You cannot change any true information that is in a credit report. You can build a new history over time, but you can't change anything that is accurate. If something is not accurate, you can certainly dispute it. But if it's true, it will remain in a credit report for up to seven years; if it's a bankruptcy, up to ten years.

Creditors Who Hassle You

Being harassed by creditors is very hurtful to women's self-esteem because they are made to feel like deadbeats. It also can feel very scary for single women living in big cities to be barraged with calls from mean people who want what little money they've managed to scrape up working.

There have been stories of young women who turn to drugs, alcohol, prostitution, or even suicide to escape their debt nightmare.

The Fair Debt Collection Practices Act protects individuals from abusive debt collection practices. The act allows consumers to dispute a debt and to stop any unreasonable collection activities, such as: calling before 8 A.M. or after 9 P.M., harassment, false statements, threatening action that is not permissible, and other unfair practices.

There are certain guidelines as to when they can call you and when they can't call you. For example, they can't call you at work if you have informed them that you can't receive personal calls at work. If they do not comply with these requests, then they commit a breach of the Fair Debt Collection Practices Act. Some states also have provisions that go beyond what the federal provisions allow. If the collection agency breaches the act, you can report the agency to your attorney general or contact an attorney.

If you send a letter to a collection agency advising it that you no longer want to be contacted, it is obligated to stop calling you except to inform you that you will be sued, which it can do by mail. The agency can contact you only to let you know of some additional action it is taking, but then it has to actually take that action. However, if the debt is with the original lender, a letter doesn't stop that lender from continuing to call.

Most women who have gone through this experience are much more careful the second time around. This doesn't mean that all of a sudden they are great money managers, but they do try to stay away from credit cards. If your debt gets this bad, seek refuge in Debtor's Anonymous.

Making a Settlement Offer

A settlement offer involves calling a creditor to negotiate a partial payment. For example, if a woman owes $1,000 but only has $750, she can call her creditor and settle on paying only what she has. That's a settlement.

The creditor's incentive for making this concession is that they usually get their principal back. There are certain expenses involved in sending statements every month, so accepting a settlement can be a cost-saving measure. Usually, however, they don't accept these kinds of deals unless you are delinquent and past due on your payments. Another possibility is when creditors believe you might be filing for bankruptcy. They'd rather take a settlement now because they risk getting much less in bankruptcy court.

One thing to be aware of with settlements: They are reported to credit bureaus, meaning that the fact you paid less than the amount that you charged is on your permanent credit record and could be viewed as a strike against your credit history.

The Seven-year Myth

The myth is that after seven years of delinquent debt, one's obligations are erased. Don't disappear to France for seven years because there are technicalities to consider. A student loan is federally insured and generally not dischargeable in bankruptcy. In many states, wages will be garnished to pay for student loans.

Department stores, for example, that feel they are never going to get their money from negligent buyers may turn collecting over to a collection agency. They can try to collect on it for seven more years. There are ways for agencies to have your debt prolonged. They can sue you and enter a judgment against you in court. Each state has different rules for how long a judgment is good. Rules for student loan debt also vary state to state. For those, collectors may garnish your income tax refund or wages.

Staying Out of Debt

The key to staying out of debt is to stick to a livable spending plan. If not, you may just run up debt all over again. Again, identify everything you spend money on and bring these expenses in line with your income.

The secret for getting out of debt—and staying clean—is sticking to a budget!

So, once you have a listing of a few months of your expenditures, sit down and create a spending plan.

Use cash for purchases as much as possible, and never make a purchase using debt or credit that you can't pay off in two to three months.

Approach staying out of debt like any other life challenge, such as losing weight, running a marathon, or getting your perfect job. Small actions every day add up to a big payoff in the long term.

Setting short- and long-term goals can help prevent debt. A short-term goal could be anything from zero to five months, or maybe for the first time setting a spending plan for Christmas. Girls, ask yourselves: How much do I spend every year on Christmas gifts? What do you spend on holiday entertaining? This also holds true for occasions throughout the year, such as birthdays and wed-

dings. Set a limit—say $1,500 a year—for what you can realisti-
cally spend on gifts.

The same holds true for the most unanticipated expense: car
repairs.

Women should be setting aside a designated amount for repairs
each month. When you're done paying off your car, continue making car payments to the bank so that you have a down payment
for the next time you have to buy a car.

Regarding long-term goals, not planning for things like a wedding will force a lot of women to pay for wedding costs with credit.
Make sure you have a cushion of at least $2,000 in your spending
plan for unexpected expenses and long-term goals.

Resources to Get Out of Debt

Debtors Anonymous: *www.debtorsanonymous.org* for a group in your
   city.

How to Get Out of Debt, Stay Out of Debt and Live Prosperously by
   Jerrold Mundis, Bantam Books, April 1990.

National Foundation for Credit Counseling (NFCC) (*www.nfcc.org*)
   for a list of credit counseling agencies in cities around the
   country.

Order a credit report: *www.creditreports.com* or
Equifax: 1-800-685-1111
Experian (formerly TRW): 1-888-397-3742
Trans Union: 1-800-916-8800

Now that you've faced your debt situation, it's time to learn how
to track your spending electronically. Chapter 12 will teach you
financial discipline with your computer, which will help you come
up with more dollars for debt repayment, savings, and shopping.

CHAPTER 12

....

Computer Cash

Why Single City Women Spend More Money

Picture yourself tooling down a city street in your spike-heeled Jimmy Choo boots and fur trimmed Givenchy coat. Suddenly you see a red Chanel suit that would go well with the Manolo Blahniks you bought last week. Ka-ching! That's an easy $250 at a designer resale shop. You're two blocks from home when a sidewalk sale catches your eye. A pink paisley purse would make a perfect gift for your favorite best friend, because we always have more than one best friend! Bling-bling: $40! Finally, you've made it to your block until you notice a new sushi restaurant. Swipe: $20 for dinner. There's no money left over to hang out tonight, so you might as well pick up a couple of fashion magazines for $10 at the newsstand. You've just spent $320 in forty-five minutes!

Cash slips through our fingers when we live in big cities because there are just so many ways to spend money—on looking good or dining or going out.

There are more clothing stores, more social events, more theaters, and a plethora of restaurants to choose from, to name just a few of the temptations that plague us big-city girls.

As a result, we lose focus and become distracted by potential purchases. The more distractions, the less likely we're able to concentrate on making and managing money. It takes focus to manage, save, and grow cash.

One way to combat the constant outflow of cash is to keep copious records. Buy a small notebook and write down every expenditure you make on a daily basis. Add it up at the end of the month. You'll never again wonder where your money went.

Downside of Vagueness

Women in their twenties and thirties have a lot to worry about, what with working out and eating right. For many of us, money is the last frontier. It's the one area we allow ourselves to run through a sunny field of daisies without a care in the world. We want to be footloose with our money because we're so disciplined about everything else. We go to the gym, we avoid sugar, we stopped engaging in one-night stands, so what else is left? "Let me have my Manolos," says a loud voice in our minds.

That's really the wrong attitude to take. Being vague about your money will only result in you not having any or in overspending what you do have.

....

Example

Rachel Sylva, a freelance graphic designer, comes across money sporadically whenever she gets a gig. Her income can vary from $2,000 one month to $15,000 the next. The twenty-eight-year-old lives in Atlanta in a beautiful Buckhead apartment, but she's had to borrow money from friends and family a few times to make ends meet.

Her problem is that she spends her money on fun things, such as shopping and entertainment, before she takes care of necessities, such as health insurance and rent.

"Just last month I found myself sitting on the floor in my apartment wondering where my money went," she said. "I didn't have money for food or a bottle of water. I was grounded!"

Rachel was surprised when her tax preparer told her she had made $60,000 last year because she was always broke.

"It seems like every time I get a check I'm having to pay back rent or the phone bill for the last three months," she said. "I'm not in debt but I'm an overspender."

....

Rachel could learn a thing or two from Christina Rohall, who uses Quicken to track her finances.

....

Example

Christina Rohall's life was full of deprivation until she started to track her expenses with computer software. Whenever she saw a designer dress she liked, she denied herself the pleasure.

"I always said to myself: I can't afford it. In actuality, if I would have budgeted better I could have afforded certain things. I was just unclear as to how much money I had," she said.

As a result of inputting her expenses into Quicken software for the past two years, the twenty-five-year-old has been able to afford nicer makeup, clothing, hair products, and other items that are icing on the cake in her active life as a single woman in California.

"I'm able to afford luxury items that I never really could afford before because I was always trying to keep up. Also, I travel a lot now. I've never been able to pay in cash for my travel expenses, and paying it up front is a great feeling," she said, adjusting her eyeglasses.

Another side benefit of knowing exactly where every red cent goes is that Christina has stopped getting into debt, and her credit card balance has stayed the same instead of growing uncontrollably.

She also uses Excel spreadsheets to give herself an idea how much money she'll end up with at the end of the year. She has a certain amount allocated toward her car, entertainment, rent, and other categories.

"I know how much money I'm going to spend each month. So, it's all automatic. If I go over in one category, like entertainment, then I know I should cut back in a another area the next month. It keeps me on track," said Christina, who likes to surf and play softball in her spare time.

The senior account executive says tracking money with her computer has taught her to sit down, evaluate, and concentrate on her needs and wants. "It helps me think about what I need and why I need it, and enables me to see the cash flow on top of it and how much money I can spend because I know my limitations," she said.

....

How Software Helps

If you don't want to carry around a notebook to write down your expenses, instead keep all of your receipts and store them in a box.

At the end of the week (on a quiet Sunday night), enter those expenses into some type of personal finance software, such as Quicken or Microsoft Money.

With Pocket Quicken for the Palm, you can enter expenses into your Palm Pilot at the time of purchase and then download them to your home computer.

Personal finance software can save you time, money, and provide a sense of control over your finances. For example, Quicken offers a feature called bill reminder, which can save you late fees by reminding you to make a credit card payment.

By knowing what's in your bank account through computer software, you can save money on bounced check fees and late fees on your credit cards as well. The key is sitting down once a week to input what you spent, which helps to focus your attention on money. The more clarity you have about your money situation, the more likely you are to earn more money.

Develop Financial Discipline

You may think you're disciplined because you work out at the gym every day, but financial discipline is a different type of animal.

The way to develop financial discipline is to force yourself to sit down and look at your financial situation. If you don't have a home computer, start by keeping records on index cards—anything to get you in the habit of evaluating your money.

Like going to the gym or church, you must schedule time to keep track of your finances. Sooner or later, inputting expenses will become part of your routine.

Once you get the hang of using computer software for money, try reading financial literature to broaden your knowledge about it. Motley Fool and AOL have an electronic personal finance newsletter. Subscribe to a personal finance magazine, such as *Bloomberg Personal Finance* and daily newspapers such as *USA Today* and *Investor's Business Daily*. Make it a habit to pore over your mutual fund and 401(k) statements.

"It's not fun when you first start out with computer software. But once you start doing it you feel like a rocket, like you are going somewhere. You get this momentum going and it becomes fun," says Martha O'Brien, an accountant with Bartleson & O'Brien in Atlanta.

Like exercise, you have to get through the initial hump before you start to feel the benefits. Once you turn money management into hobby, it gets to be something you look forward to. Besides, who wouldn't want to know how much they're spending on martinis, Manolos, and manicures? You might want to buy stock in the companies that produce them!

Why It's Fun

Most personal finance software is fun and sexy. It can compete with other things that can distract you, such as Internet shopping and e-mailing friends.

Part of the battle is knowing that you need to earn $10,000 more per year, for example. The more clarity you have on your money situation, the more likely you are to earn more money.

But entering expenses into the computer can get boring over time. So, find ways to make it exciting by coming up with a short-term financial goal. Get a picture of your goal, maybe a vacation or new car, and post it on a bulletin board near your workstation.

"It's an old cliché of envisioning the reward. You can tear pictures out of your favorite magazine, get travel brochures, post them, and start shopping the reward while you are creating the financial position that's going to give you the payoff," says O'Brien. The key is creating a positive association with tracking your expenses. Add a glass of wine, a cup of tea, or light a candle—anything to make it special for yourself.

Quicken is especially easy to work with because it creates reports and graphs, such as pie charts and bar graphs based on your numbers.

For example, 50 percent of your pie may have gone to dining, 10 percent to groceries, and 30 percent to entertainment.

There's an income versus expense graph to see if you are spending more than you're earning month by month or in the past six months to a year.

A net worth graph adds up assets, subtracts liabilities, shows how you are doing over time, and shows what your net worth is.

Quicken states your checking account balances, reconciles your checkbook, and can download information directly from more than 1,700 banks around the country.

The program is intuitive. "Quicken will notice that you've made this payment called rent the first of every month and it will say: Hey, I noticed you make this payment so do you want to just set it up so you don't miss it? It reminds you," says Dan Olsen, group project manager for Quicken in California.

Quicken allows you to access your whole banking transaction history and keeps track of checks that haven't cleared. But that feature does require inputting the checks you've written. Once you've entered checks, Quicken categorizes each one.

The program will automatically create a budget for you based on your previous spending patterns. Subsequently, reports will show how you're doing relative to your budget, whether you are over-spending or underspending in each month.

Under the planning icon of the Quicken menu, you'll find the debt reduction planner, which allows you to download your credit card statements into Quicken.

It tells you your balance for each card as well as interest rates and gives you a plan on how to pay down those credit cards in a way that will save you the most money.

The software also can track all of your investments by down-loading statements from your brokerage firm. There's a tax planner, which tells whether you are getting a refund or owe money to the IRS. It also contains a tax withholding estimator to figure out whether the right amount is being taken out of your check or not.

Quicken 2001 is the current version available for both Windows and Macintosh. For Macintosh, it's called Quicken Deluxe. For Windows there is Basic, Deluxe, Deluxe Suite, Home and Business, and Home and Business Suite.

The Home and Business Suite is similar to Deluxe, but it also has some tracking tools for accounts payable, receivables, and invoicing. The difference between Basic and Deluxe is that Basic costs less and doesn't have the long-term planning (think retirement) or tax features. It does, however, contain the budgeting feature.

Websites versus Software

In addition to personal finance software, websites such as *Yodlee.com*, *Quicken.com*, and Yahoo! Finance offer personal finance tools. But women aren't avid users of the Internet for any purposes relating to saving and investing, according to the chart below.

Oppenheimer Funds asked people if they use the Internet for any purposes relating to saving and investing their money. Respondents between the ages of twenty-one and thirty-four said:

Response	Men Percentage	Women Percentage
Yes	31%	22%
No	69%	78%

When asked whether they use the Internet for any of the following purposes, respondents said:

Purpose	Men Percentage	Women Percentage
Review an investment account	64%	63%
Correspond with financial advisor	26%	20%
Buy or sell mutual funds	21%	35%
Buy or sell individual stocks	37%	44%
Research investments	79%	76%
Use financial planning software	44%	34%
Manage retirement accounts	41%	46%
Not sure	6%	9%

One reason may be that women aren't comfortable posting their whole financial life on the Web. People prefer storing info on their hardware rather than on the Web because of privacy and speed issues.

"The best combination is using both because the desktop is great at certain things and the Web is great at certain things. The desktop, for example, is still a lot faster than the Web. So if you want to run a report or you want to run a graph, it's a lot faster on the desktop hard drive versus having to sit on the Web and waiting for the page to load," says Dan Olsen.

Services such as *Yodlee.com* aggregate various personal financial data and store it in one place. You can retrieve all of your personal accounts, such as bank balance, frequent flier miles, credit card accounts, stock portfolios, 401(k) accounts, and even have access to all of your e-mail accounts from a central location.

"It gives you a holistic picture of your financial and personal life so that you can be more efficient with your time and aware of where your dollars are," says Geralyn Volk, vice president of sales at *Yodlee.com*.

If you were to click on banking, for example, you could put your Wells Fargo, CitiBank, and Bank of America checking accounts all in one place.

Gone are the days of having to memorize ten different passwords.

"At Yodlee, you enter your account number and password once and never have to enter another thing because we update it. We go out en masse for our million plus customers and gather information on 300,000 accounts for all of the CitiBank customers, for example, across the whole Yodlee network," says Volk.

You can also set up alerts that will tell when your checking account balance drops below a certain amount or when your credit card bill is due.

Yodlee is customer-controlled and can be custom-tailored. So, for example, you could just keep track of your credit card accounts without using any of the other aggregating services offered on the site.

Best of all, it's free!

Security of Finances on the Internet

Yodlee uses a number of different firewalls and encryption technology to ensure security on the Web. The site also uses intrusion detection systems and around-the-clock monitoring. But that's still not enough to convince accountant O'Brien to put all of her info in one central location on the Web.

"I wouldn't want my comprehensive data in one place because somebody could steal your identity," says O'Brien.

She adds that she would use the Internet only to manage a specific asset with a trusted financial institution.

Four Ways to Prevent Identity Theft

1. Shred every credit card offer that comes through the mail.

2. Have the hard drives of old computers and laptops reformatted and erased.

3. Don't let other people have access to your home computer.

4. Add security to your home computer, such as firewalls and online virus scanning. Visit *www.deerfieldpd.com* for a personal firewall.

Now that you've used the computer to get your accounts straight, Chapter 13 discusses how to leverage various portfolios, including stocks, 401(k) plans, and insurance policies.

CHAPTER 13

··

Borrowing Against Tomorrow for Today

Big-City Perks

Major corporations are more likely to be located in big cities than in smaller towns. As a result, single women working at big companies in metro areas may get perks that women in smaller towns don't have access to. For example, larger companies may offer stock options and deferred compensation benefit plans. The trade-off is that those living in smaller towns at smaller companies may be able to work more flexible hours.

Leveraging the assets of your big-city job is one of the best-kept secrets.

You can borrow from your 401(k), IRA, stock portfolio, and cash-value life insurance. But each one has different restrictions. This chapter teaches you how to borrow from each of these assets. Of course, it's always better to operate on a cash basis and avoid borrowing. But in every single woman's life there's at least one emergency that requires quick cash. Whether it's for a plane ticket or designer gown for a charity ball, the rule of thumb is: Pay it back.

Borrowing from Stock Portfolios

As appealing as the new runway clothes may be, that's the wrong reason to leverage your account. Save it for an absolute emergency, such as a Death-in-the-Family plane ticket. But really, if you don't have to borrow, don't.

A leveragable account is a portfolio of individual investments containing stocks and bonds. Margining is the ability to use your investments as collateral to borrow against them without selling securities. Not all investments are marginable. For example, annuities cannot be margined.

Margin rules are federally regulated, but margin requirements and interest may vary among broker-dealers. When working with a broker-dealer, your account statement will show the marginable level, or what you can borrow.

Borrowing and margining are essentially the same thing but with different operational issues. When borrowing from a bank, you have to prepare documents, be approved, and service the loan, which involves paying interest regularly.

With margining, you can write a check for the loan amount if your account allows margining. You don't have to pay interest, but interest accrues on the debit balance and is paid at the time the margin loan is paid off.

"Think of it as an extra allowance that at some point you are going to have to pay back. There's nothing that's costing you anything because you're not getting a bill every month with an interest charge. The problem comes up when every time you need extra money, you just write a check. That's not the way to use margining," says David Speck, managing director at First Union Securities.

Under the rules of borrowing and margining, generally you can take out 50 percent of the value of your account in cash. For example, if you have a $100,000 portfolio of stocks and bonds, you can write out a check for $50,000.

The account accrues interest when you start borrowing against it. The interest is tax deductible because it is investment interest, but it is subject to certain restrictions. A tax advisor can address each individual situation.

Unlike 401(k) plans, people are never required to pay back their margin debt unless they wish to close the account or the account falls below the equity maintenance requirement. Remember, however, you will constantly be racking up margin interest, which is usually at prime. The interest rate decreases as the amount of margin debt increases. There is also no tax penalty for borrowing against your stock portfolio.

Margining is often the interim step before liquidating some securities. People generally choose to margin rather than sell because the market and tax situation is down in that particular moment or because they are expecting a large sum of money within the year with which to pay it back.

When margining, you have to be sure that your debt doesn't get too large or more than the amount of the basic asset value. If not, "you face a margin call," says Speck. Once margined, if the value of the stock drops sufficiently, the owner will be asked either to put in more cash or to sell a portion of the stock. This is a margin call, which simply means that debt has exceeded the available ratio of debt to asset value. You must either deliver cash or securities or sell something, sometimes within twenty-four hours.

If your account is made up mostly of technology stocks, you can easily expect to have a margin call. If your portfolio consists of solid blue-chip companies, you could see some volatility but you're not going to jeopardize your underlying values, according to Speck.

Don't think of margining your portfolio as a cookie jar. You want to plan and prepare leveraging and not let it become a hole that gets deeper. If you are going to margin, think about how you are going to repay or risk being caught red-handed.

The way to use margining is to look at what your monetary need is compared to your total assets. Think about margining in the context of the size of the assets, the size of your borrowing, and the circumstances of your borrowing.

Aim to pay back what you borrowed at the end of the month because margining from your stock portfolio is for short-term needs.

There's a big difference between borrowing $2,000 from an account worth $50,000 and borrowing $2,000 from an account that contains only $10,000. In the latter example, $2,000 is 20 percent of the portfolio.

As a general rule, don't borrow from your portfolio unless you have at least $10,000.

"Even then I would advise not to be doing much borrowing because of the risks of getting a margin call. I would be very cautious," says David Bendix of the Bendix Financial Group. "If you borrow this money and the stock market tanks, you have to replace it. So, where are you going to get the money?"

There is a lot of risk involved in margining, but if you need easy short-term money at a reasonable interest rate, you can get a very good rate through margining your stock portfolio. Speck advises not to margin outstanding money for more than a year and ideally less than a month.

Pros of Borrowing from a Stock Portfolio

- Very competitive rates that can be better than a credit card or an unsecured bank loan
- No paperwork involved
- No payback scenario
- Deductible interest
- No tax penalty

Cons of Borrowing from a Stock Portfolio

- Interest accrues
- At the mercy of market volatility

- Risk of a margin call

- Having to come up with cash from another place in the event of a margin call

....

Example

Los Angeles resident Kathy Sills was given 5,000 shares of company stock as a gift from a wealthy relative. Each share was worth $20 for a total value of $100,000. The thirty-year-old margined $50,000, which was 50 percent of the market value of the portfolio.

Kathy used the money partly to pay for cosmetic surgery. The actress had breast implants, a tummy tuck, a thigh lift, and a nose job.

She recovered physically within three months but not financially. After six months, her stock suddenly dropped to $14 per share.

Her broker phoned to tell her that her account was only worth $70,000. Since she had borrowed $50,000, the debit balance was now at 30 percent. She experienced a margin call.

The Philadelphia native couldn't come up with the money to buy more securities, so she had to sell out the account to retire the margin.

"It really killed me to do that. I'm only left with $20,000, and to think that I had $100,000 eighteen months ago," she said. The scars on her body from the cosmetic surgery are not nearly as unsightly as a drained portfolio.

....

Although a repayment plan is not a requirement of margining your stock portfolio, it is a good idea to create a plan. Even if the plan is simply committing to paying back the loan six months from now or selling some of your stock to cover the loan, you should have some kind of repayment plan in mind.

Retirement Accounts

IRAs, 401(k)s, and annuities cannot be margined. At best, you can take money out of an IRA, and put it back in within 60 days, and not be taxed or penalized. You can borrow up to 50 percent of the value of a 401(k) but never more than $50,000, but that's not considered margining. When borrowing from a 401(k), you must establish a repayment plan. The good news is that your loan is not affected by changing market values. The bad news is you cannot roll over your 401(k) if you change jobs without paying back the loan first, and the interest on a 401(k) is not deductible. Set up a repayment plan with your plan provider or administrator.

Borrowing from 401(k) Plans

If you've been following the suggestions in this book, you shouldn't have to borrow from your retirement accounts. Borrowing from your 401(k) plan should be your last resort because the plan is set up to provide you with money in retirement, not in the present moment. Now that you've been forewarned, here's the scoop on borrowing.

Before borrowing from your 401(k), evaluate your job situation to determine whether it's secure. You don't want to be in a situation where you are fired within three months of borrowing from your plan; if you lose your job, you'll have to pay back the loan immediately. If you don't pay it back, you are assessed penalties because it's deemed a distribution.

To secure a loan, call your human resources department or the plan administrator to get a loan request form. Your payback is usually a monthly payment over five years.

Some companies may have restrictions on how soon you can borrow from your 401(k) plan. If you're new, you may have to wait two years to borrow. Other companies require you to work for the company for a year before you contribute to the 401(k) plan.

Some plans may have a one-time borrowing fee. For example, they may charge $35 to $50 or an annual maintenance fee of $20 a year.

··

Example

Judy Tucker borrowed money from her 401(k) plan in order to take a monthlong sabbatical in Greece. As creative director at a magazine, she was able to convince higher-ups that she needed time off to refresh her mind for creative ideas. But getting time off was only half the battle. The thirty-five-year-old had to figure out how to fund the trip.

Judy borrowed $5,000 from her 401(k) with the intent of making monthly payments over a three-year period.

Upon her return from Greece, she faithfully made monthly payments of $140 toward her loan while continuing to make $150 contributions to her plan. But after three months, she was having difficulty forking over nearly $300 toward her plan. Her contributions faltered so that she could continue to repay the loan.

As a result, she lost out on matching contributions from her company for thirty-four months.

"I didn't think about having to make contributions while paying back the loan," she said. "That really threw my budget off."

··

If you're borrowing from your 401(k), make sure you're in a position to pay back the loan and continue to make contributions so that you don't miss out on your employer's matching contribution.

Pros of Borrowing from 401(k) Plans

- Easy access. There are no credit check requirements prior to getting the loan.

- You are paying interest to yourself through the account, so it's really not costing you anything.

Cons

- If you decide to leave the company and you can't pay back the loan, the loan will be considered a taxable distribution and you'll face premature penalties.

- The interest isn't deductible.

- If the market does well, you could miss out on market returns while the money is out of your account. Better to have $10,000 compounding in the stock market than not.

- In some cases, there are one-time borrowing fees and/or annual maintenance fees.

If you are under age fifty-nine and a half, the money you withdraw from your 401(k) plan will be taxed immediately by the IRS, and a 10 percent penalty is assessed on the amount you've withdrawn. If you borrow without paying back, it's considered a withdrawal and you become subject to penalties and taxes.

So if Sue Ellen borrows $2,000 and then can't pay back the loan, she will pay full taxes on that $2,000 dollars and the IRS will impose an extra $200 penalty.

"Most people tend to never pay it back because if they needed the money to borrow they are not going to have the money to pay it back. That is the last place that I recommend people go to tap into their money," says Wendy Ehrlich, vice-president of sales at Oppenheimer Funds. "Just like credit card debt, it can become an albatross around your neck."

Borrowing from Your 401(k) versus Borrowing from Your Stock Portfolio

Deciding whether to margin your stock portfolio or borrow from your 401(k) plan depends on how much is in each account and what your borrowing needs are. Some experts recommend forgoing both in favor of a home equity line of credit.

Home Equity Line of Credit

When you take out a home equity line of credit, you are borrowing against the equity in your home—provided that you own a home.

With a home equity line of credit, you apply for a lump-sum amount but do not pay interest on the loan until you start to write checks against the loan. The rate on this type of a loan is at least prime, which varies. The good news is the interest payments on home equity loans and home equity lines of credit are tax-deductible.

Borrowing from Individual Retirement Accounts

You can't borrow from an IRA but you can take advantage of the 60-day rollover rule. You can withdraw money for sixty days, but then you have to put it back into the IRA account. If you don't replace it after sixty days, the full amount will be taxed and you'll pay a 10 percent penalty.

With $100,000, you could set up four $25,000 IRA accounts and then take out $25,000, use it for 60 days, then take $25,000 from another IRA, and replace it in the first one.

"You're wrapping it so you can kind of stretch out the sixty-day period and have use of the money without any of the tax or

interest costs or penalties," says Bendix. "Not a lot of people uti-
lize this, but it's a nice concept."

There are exceptions to IRA withdrawal rules. You can take
money out for a first-home purchase or for educational purposes
with some restrictions.

Life Insurance Policies

Borrowing from Life Insurance Policies

Ever wonder what to do with that life insurance policy? Psst, girls,
it may not be so useless after all if you learn how to leverage your
cash value policy. But again, borrowing from any account should
be your last resort.

When you borrow from an insurance company, you are pledg-
ing the cash value of your account as collateral. The advantage is
that the loan rate tends to be very reasonable.

"Usually what happens is the insurance company will charge you
eight percent but they credit your account for six percent. The cost
is two percentage points. So it's pretty cost-efficient," says Bendix.

Another advantage is easy access. There is no requirement for
providing credit resources because the loan is backed by the poli-
cyholder's interest in the life insurance policy. It's a very simple,
noncomplicated process. In addition, the interest rates are generally market-based. Ask the insurance company to send you the
proper form to fill out. After you send it in, they send you a check.

The disadvantage is people generally buy insurance to provide
an estate for an heir, but when you borrow and don't pay back, the
outstanding part of the loan and any accumulated interest will be
deducted from the death benefit.

"It's a question of balancing your need for current cash versus
your interest in providing a death benefit. That would be a very

individual decision," says William Schreiner, actuary with the American Council of Life Insurers in Washington, D.C.

Types of Policies to Borrow From

You can borrow from permanent insurance policies. They include traditional fixed-premium life insurance policies, such as whole life, variable life, and universal life, which are cash-value policies.

"If you bought permanent insurance, it is there to carry you from now until the end of life. It generates cash value," says Schreiner.

Generally, with traditional fixed-premium insurance, you have to send a specified premium to the insurance company to keep the insurance enforced. That is a level premium throughout life, which creates cash values that can be borrowed against.

Term insurance, which is insurance for a specific period of time, does not develop cash values to borrow from.

Tax Issues of Borrowing from Life Insurance Policies

The good news is there are no tax consequences to borrowing money from a life insurance policy until you get to the point where you have taken out more from the policy than you have put in. There could be tax consequences if the policy lapses with an outstanding balance. But the only way the policy can lapse is if you stop making premium payments.

Repayment of Life Insurance Policies

Another advantage is that there is no requirement to repay the loan at any time. You can merely let the loan accumulate interest, which only reduces the death benefit.

Overall, there is no schedule requirement for repayment because the loan is secured by the value of the policy. But it could reach a point where the loan eats up the value in the policy and you have to put money into the policy or else the policy terminates.

Borrowing Limits to Insurance Policies

The borrowing limit is the amount of the cash value that you have in the policy.

You can get out of the policy nearly the entire cash value of the loan, or the cash value less the interest you would have to pay that year.

Other Company Benefits that Big-City Women Have at Major Corporations

An employer stock purchase plan is simply a discount on the purchase price of the stock of the employer. A stock option is a contract that allows the holder to buy a specific amount of stock at a specific price for a specific amount of time. You cannot leverage a stock purchase plan or deferred compensation plan.

Now that you know how to borrow against tomorrow for today in case of an emergency, Chapter 14 explains how to spend less money during your leisure time so that you won't ever have to leverage your investments or retirement accounts.

CHAPTER 14

....

Ladies Who Lunch
Without Loot

On *Sex and the City*, Samantha, Carrie, Miranda, and Charlotte brunch in hip restaurants for a debriefing on what's new, or, ahem, not new in their sex lives. Ever wonder where they get the money? In addition to lunch in trendy eateries, single urban women who frequent charity events and jet-set around the world face the same dilemma: how to pay for their glamorous lifestyle. This chapter gives ideas on how to lunch without loot, party without paying, and vacation without emptying your wallet.

Charity Events

Why Charity?

Living in cities can be isolating and lonely. The more you can make yourself part of something, the better off you'll be socially.

Charity work can fill lonely Saturday afternoons and help you make new friends who have something in common: a desire to better the world. Getting involved in charity work can be a great introduction to life in the big city you've chosen and its issues. In addition, volunteering can give you new job skills.

Charity organizations host big fund-raisers that appeal to the upwardly mobile professional class, but they also tend to cost a pretty penny. Be prepared to spend a hundred bucks for a party unless you're connected.

Check out *www.CityCares.org*, an organization that offers volunteer opportunities and monthly social activities. It has chapters in twenty-three cities, including Boston, Baltimore, Detroit, Miami, and Nashville.

The way to get connected is simple: get involved.

There's usually an inner circle within the inner circle of charity committees. Invitations to the smaller social cocktail mixers and meetings are issued to those who are active in the organization rather than those who just attend events.

There are so many charities to choose from, so where should you commit?

Wherever you are more comfortable is where you'll find the most success. Suffice it to say that there is no shortage of options.

"When you call to inquire about volunteer opportunities, ask for the person who oversees the young professionals division or the new leadership development area," says Robin Gorman Newman, a love coach in Manhattan and founder of *www.LoveCoach.com*.

Being on the party planning committee can be fun because you help organize some of the fund-raisers.

Affording Charity Events

Not only do charity events often cost upward of $100 for a ticket, but you also have to dress the part. That means buying a cocktail dress or gown for the more formal occasions.

A good enough reason to volunteer is that you can get reduced admission. If you can't get in for free, ask for a discount.

••

Example

Calister Freeman, a twenty-seven-year-old Boston professional, isn't a trust fund baby, but you wouldn't know it. The petite blonde is active in the

Public Auction for the Arts organization, which raises money for educational programs for children in theater and the arts. Many charities have put her name on their invitations to attract a particular kind of crowd.

"They'll ask you if you will lend them your name to put on the invitation and then you get a free invitation for yourself and a couple of guests," Calister said. "That's if you are part of the cool crowd."

So how did she get into the cool crowd? Calister started her charity career crashing events.

"You show up in the lobby of these events dressed to kill. Then walk up to a man and ask to take his arm as you're strolling in. Usually they stamp your arm or they put a wristband on you," Calister said. "The trick is walking in with your head held high so that no one will question you."

She has met multimillionaires, presidents of Fortune 500 companies, and trust fund babies, many of them nice men.

"People look at the charity circuit as a safe way to go and meet people. But you never want people to know that you crashed a party even though a lot of these people do the same thing. It's not something to boast about," she said.

Calister's favorite events are Christmas parties when organizations ask you to buy a ticket or bring a toy. "You can always buy a nice-looking china doll for fifteen dollars," she said.

During high season (fall, winter, spring), the city cyclist is known to frequent four events a week.

The regular churchgoer at St. Stephen's in Boston's North End can't afford a new dress each night, so she discount shops and recycles her dresses. Calister's favorite store to raid for cocktail dresses is Filene's Basement. She repeats dresses by adding a scarf and interesting jewelry. As scarves can get expensive, she trades them with her girlfriends.

"I've worn a dress three nights in a row. I have this vintage Matthew Johnson that I wear with a red scarf around my neck, and then I will wear it the next night with a green sweater over it. Then I'll wear it the next night with a man's white shirt tied at my waist in a Daisy Mae knot, different shoes and jewelry, and you get totally different looks," she said.

The ski bunny wore a silk scarf wrapped around her chest as a shirt once when she had no money to do laundry. Calister also has been known to wear a turquoise scarf in her hair as a turban and on another night wear two pigtail braids.

"People think I am a rich girl because I am always very well dressed. They don't know that I'm a working girl," says Calister, giggling.

● ●

Junior Boards

Charitable organizations often have junior boards that are put together specifically to target professionals under the age of thirty-five. The idea behind it is to groom the next leadership group and get people involved at an early age.

Every junior board is different, but some can be very exclusive and require an invitation to join. Others carry a monetary responsibility or a minimum contribution each year. The way to get invited is to know somebody who is already on the board.

Mistakes of Charity Work

- *Overcommitting yourself.* There are a lot of demands for volunteer services. You have to be careful not to spread yourself too thin.

- *Not getting training.* Many volunteer organizations offer training for their volunteers. Take advantage.

- *Being afraid of unfamiliar territory.* Maybe you've never had any exposure to the inner city. Nevertheless, don't let your fears get in the way of rewarding new experiences.

- *Insincerity.* Don't make it obvious that you came there only to meet people. Select a cause you care about. For example, if your mother survived breast cancer, you may want to do some work for a breast cancer charity.

- *Being misinformed about your charity of choice.* Educate yourself about the organization. Make sure you are comfortable with the nature of their fund-raising.

Meet Men through Charity Events

The more you're out there, the more likely you will meet a mate. If you meet a man doing charity work, at least you know he has a heart.

"It's no guarantee that you will meet your husband, but you will encounter new friends who may lead you to your next boyfriend. It's all about networking," says love coach Newman.

Sporting events that are sponsored by charity organizations attract athletic men who care about their bodies and their health. For example, the Multiple Sclerosis Society hosts bike tours in various cities around the country, including New York City and San Antonio. For more information on the MS Bike Tour in your city, call the MS Bike Tour Hotline at 212-463-9791 or visit *www.msnyc.org.* If you can't run a marathon or bike for miles, you can volunteer on the day of the race to give out water to the runners and bikers, which increases your chance of meeting other volunteers.

Men often travel from big city to big city to run in marathons.

Don't shy away if your charitable organization asks you to sell raffle tickets. Take them to your office, the gym, your apartment building and alumni association. It's a great excuse to start up a conversation. Before you sign on to sell tickets, educate yourself about the organization through their membership brochures or the Internet so that you can have a conversation when people ask for more details.

∙∙∙

Example

At thirty-four, Gwenn Lezard has been married three years. Prior to meeting her husband, she volunteered for the party planning committee of a few charitable organizations in Dallas.

During a New Year's Eve fund-raising party for a children's charity, Gwenn volunteered to give out party favors.

"I didn't have to come up with a line because my job was to talk to people. I approached every cute guy and gave him a horn to blow. It was a perfect excuse," she said.

That night, Gwenn gave a paper hat to a hot guy whom she later dated and married.

"My husband said he never would have asked me out if I hadn't approached him first about the party favors!"

∙∙∙

Starting Your Own Nonprofit

Starting your own nonprofit for a cause that's close to your heart is another good way to meet men. After all, you have to create a board of directors that you glean from Wall Street, Hollywood, or your city's Chamber of Commerce. But it won't be easy. On the contrary, it will take a lot of effort to get all the necessary paperwork together. Nothing worthwhile is ever easy. Here are the eight steps to starting your own nonprofit organization:

1. File an article of incorporation to legally establish the name and purpose of your nonprofit organization.

2. Create bylaws that act as the organization's governing document, defining how the nonprofit will be managed and operated.

3. Apply for tax-exempt status by filing Form 1023 with the IRS, or download it from *www.irs.ustreas.gov.*

4. Apply for an employer identification number by filing Form SS-4.

5. Recruit a board of directors, which should have at least three members. Look for diverse skills and experience when recruiting directors.

6. Write a mission statement. This is your organization's reason for being in a few sentences.

7. Develop a budget. How much will it cost to rent office space, buy office equipment, set up a phone line, and advertise?

8. Find funding. This is the hard part. Your charity can provide services for funding, apply for foundation and government grants, organize fund-raising events, and appeal to the masses for money. The key is to ask.

Jet-Setting on a Budget

If all your charity work doesn't pay off in the man department, your fate may lie elsewhere. It's time to think about traveling to other cities and countries because Mr. Right may not live in your city. He may be a construction worker in Maine, a graduate student in Idaho, or a first-grade teacher in Brazil. Dust off your rolling suitcase and put on your traveling shoes!

When single, urban women travel, they're not after the basic art gallery in Paris, France, or the typical long relaxing weekend in Santa Fe. No, they want the nitty gritty: adventure travel. We opt for climbing at Kathmandu, trekking in Wales, rock-climbing in the Pacific Northwest, kayaking, rappelling, mountain biking, camping, and hiking because it helps us express our independence.

About 60 percent of the solo adventure traveler market is composed of single women, according to a study issued by Euro RSCG, a marketing communications firm.

"They look for respites that really turn them on. The real adventure stuff appeals to single women," says Marian Salzman, global director of planning and strategy at Euro RSCG in New York.

Either way, jet-setting, whether it's for man-hunting or scaling a mountain, can get very expensive. So, what's a hip gal to do? Instead of going to the passenger terminals at the airport, go to the UPS, FedEx, and Fly Tigers offices to hitchhike by air.

Bonnie Russell, a marketing director and experienced discount traveler, advises hanging out in the courier lobby and gabbing with everyone you meet until you get invited to accompany the pilot on a flight.

"It's fun because you can pick off the pilots right away, and they generally go to hubs. That is how you can go places," she said. "You are the package honey!" That's a strategy that only Samantha can appreciate.

Discount Courier Travel

There are legitimate ways to fly for free that don't require flirting, namely courier travel and seat forfeiture.

The way courier travel works is air freight companies subsidize tickets for couriers. The air freight company buys a ticket and charges the courier less than market price. In return, the courier accompanies the package through customs. Otherwise, if it's not passenger-accompanied baggage, the package can sit for days or weeks before it clears customs.

The more popular the destination, the less the subsidy, says Edward Hasbrouck of *www.Airtecks.com* in San Francisco.

"They want to buy you the cheapest possible ticket, which means flying round trip with a short stay for a fixed schedule because they want to arrange one courier to go there and come back," Hasbrouck said. "It's not good if you're going to a tourist destination during tourist season, not good if you want to stay a long time, and not good if you're not coming from a big city."

Courier travel isn't what it's cracked up to be, but for some people it can work well. About 80 percent of all courier flights originate out of New York City, flying to Europe, South America, and Asia. Other courier flights fly out of Los Angeles, Miami, San Francisco, and Chicago. From Miami, most courier flights are headed to South America. From L.A., expect to go to the South Pacific. If Asia is your goal, you're most likely to fly from San Francisco and L.A.

Keep in mind that when flying as a courier, you'll be traveling alone.

Giving Up Your Seat

If you have the flexibility, you can get a free plane ticket by giving up your previously purchased seat. Get to the airport early so that you can upgrade.

"There are some seats that are only assigned at check-in, and you may be able to get a better seat than the one you had. For example, some exit rows are only assigned at check-in," says Hasbrouck.

When you check in, ask the clerk to put you on the list as a volunteer. Getting bumped is first come, first served. The earlier you get to the airport, the higher up on the list you will be.

Putting yourself on the list doesn't commit you; it just gives you the opportunity to see if the compensation is worth it.

....

Example

Stacy Solovey, a manager at the Venetian Resort and Casino in Las Vegas, paid $580 for a flight to Spain on www.Travelocity.com *because she was flexible with her departure dates.*

"I went the second week in April. Because it was off-peak season, I got cheaper tickets," she said.

Stacy frequented hostels, which are small hotels, in various cities in Spain, spending about $800 for eight nights. When she lodged in hotels, she was given a discount of $20 to $30 because she was alone. Stacy lowered her food bill by taking advantage of the free breakfast that many hotels offer, spending about $300 on food during her eight-day stay.

"The good thing about Europe, at least for Spain, is that they have their big meal during the day. I would get the free breakfast from the hotel and at about 2:00 p.m. or 3:00 P.M., I would have a large lunch, the menu of the day, for about $15," she said. "At night, I would have a snack. I didn't eat all that much."

Another way to save was using ATM machines rather than her credit cards or traveler's checks in order to get a better exchange rate.

....

Stacy didn't spend more than $2,500, a steal for a weeklong visit to Europe.

Ways to Save on Your Vay-kay

- When lodging in hotel rooms, request a fridge so that you can buy food from a grocery store and eat in rather than at expensive restaurants. If no fridge is available, ask hotel staff to empty the minibar and stock up with food from a local grocery store.

- Eat at places that have buffets, and take leftovers from your plate home for the next day. Take advantage of early-bird dinner specials, which are often cheaper.

- The cost of travel is a function of local wage scales. Choose destinations that are not so expensive. Even a skillful savvy budget traveler will have a hard time traveling as cheaply in an expensive country, such as in Western Europe, as compared to poorer countries, such as in Southeast Asia or South America. It may take longer and more money to travel to Bali or Peru, but upon arrival cost of living will be cheaper, especially for a longer vacation.

- Travel during off-peak seasons.

- Go to less-traveled places at less-traveled times; for example, Nantucket at Christmas or the Carribean during hurricane season in August. Going where other people aren't can save you a lot of money.

- Avoid marquee attractions. The cost adds up unless they are free.

- Be spontaneous. It gives you the opportunity to take advantage of unanticipated opportunities that present themselves, such as a free meal with a handsome Italian in Rome. You pay a price for having things planned out.

- Don't use debt to finance your trip. Coming back from a trip and having to go back to work is bad enough without having to face added debt. Save up the money ahead of time.

- Opt for youth hostels rather than hotels. They're a great place to meet other young, single travelers to partner up with. Be prepared for dorm-style accommodations, however.

- Save money by telling hotel managers abroad that you're alone. In some cases, they'll cut a few dollars off your day rate.

- Buy travel insurance because most medical insurance policies don't cover health problems when you're overseas. It costs about $70 and can be purchased on the Internet.

- Travel by rail rather than air. You can cut your fare in half if you're willing to forfeit time on the train.

Creating a Travel Budget

Bigger money problems come from not planning. Create a budget for your trip and plan to stick to it. Things to include in your budget are cost of transportation once you've arrived at your destination, food, sightseeing (museum admissions, for example), shopping, and new clothes for the trip. Factor in a $100 cushion for unexpected expenses.

···

Example

Chantelle Bell had $800 for a quick getaway out of her cramped Manhattan apartment. She opted for Nantucket, a Massachusetts island. Round-trip transportation from New York to Boston by train cost her $131, $27 for round-trip bus transportation from Boston to Cape Cod, and $48 round-trip for ferry rides to and from Nantucket.

"The trip took a full eight hours whereas if I'd flown it would have taken all of two hours. But I saved money and used the time to get some work done," Chantelle said.

Once on the quaint island, Chantelle spent $400 for five nights at a bed and breakfast and $63 to rent a bicycle from the Holiday Bike Shop. Instead of eating in the pricey restaurants, she opted to dine in on pepperoni, olives, pickles, tuna, sardines, and tomatoes that she purchased at the grocery store.

"It really would have been nice to eat a lobster or two, but I was on a budget," she said.

The money she saved on food, she spent on $5 taxi rides and night-time entertainment.

Chantelle incurred one unexpected cost. It was colder than she expected on the island so she bought a red Nantucket sweatshirt for $38 and paid $25 for a boat ride on the Endeavor, *a sailboat.*

"I had to allow myself a little treat," she said. "After all, it was a vacation, even if it was only six days," she said.

Overall, Chantelle spent no more than $800 for a six-day getaway, two days of which were spent traveling.

· ·

Five Great Travel Destinations for Singles

The Burning Man Festival, August 26–September 2, 2002: *www.burningman.com*

Club Med's Turks and Caicos: *www.vacation-travel.com/turk.htm*

The Sonesta Resort, June 9-16: *www.arubasonesta.com*

Bike Trips for Singles: *www.backroads.com* or 1-800-GO-ACTIVE

Singles Cruises: *www.singlescruise.com, www.cruising.org, www.singles-cruise.com, www.singlescruises-tour.com*

Summer Shares

Some of us are lucky enough to rest our pretty heads as guests at huge estates in the Hamptons or on Cape Cod, but for those who aren't quite connected, there's the imfamous summer share.

Like MTV's *Real World*, summer shares can be intense but also a great way to make new friends and broaden your social circle. Not only are you in a relaxing atmosphere, you're in a group home situation that can result in bonding and summer fun. The smaller the number of people in the house, the better the "family" dynamic. Whether you're in Newport, Rhode Island, Martha's Vineyard, Nantucket, or the Hamptons, New York, a summer share is definitely something you want to experience at least once. Here are some tips to make it more economically feasible on a working girl's salary.

Tips for Summer Shares

1. Opt for a quarter share rather than a full or half share. A full share means that you come out to the house every weekend. A half share allows you access every other weekend, and a quarter gives you four to six weekends, depending on the house.

2. Guest at different houses. It's often cheaper to be a guest of various friends four or five times in a summer than paying for a share at the beginning of the summer.

3. Bring your own food so that you won't have to pitch in for the house food.

4. Get around on a bicycle instead of renting a car.

5. Be a house manager so that you get the benefits of a full share for free.

....

Example

As house manager of an eight-bedroom Southampton share house in New York, Kelley Greenier gets a free summer share and the opportunity to make new friends. The disadvantage is that it's a lot more work than she antic-ipated. The social worker has to be present for every happy hour prior to Memorial Day in order to recruit house members.

"In April and May we were doing three happy hours a week, and it took a huge bite out of my social life. It's not like I could just sit back with a beer and relax. I had to be on. It sounds like fun but it was work," she said.

Part of being a house manager is acting as social coordinator. The twenty-seven-year-old is often worried about other people's happiness.

"I want everybody to be happy and not everybody is going to be happy in the share house. There are rules that I am there to enforce and not every-body likes them."

The opportunity fell into her lap unexpectedly.

"I was at a charity benefit with my girlfriend and she introduced me to the owner of the house. He asked me to come look at the house and the next thing I know he's telling me I have a full summer share in exchange for managing and recruiting people," she said.

A full share in the house would cost her $5,500. The leggy blonde is paying the price in responsibility.

"I spend about three to five hours a week e-mailing people, processing guest requests, dealing with lost and found. People call with questions or they want to switch weekends and I have to keep up with all of that," she said. "I also have to collect the guest fees and go grocery shopping with that money. It's a pain having to buy food for thirty people."

Despite playing watchdog, Kelley doesn't regret the move. "I definitely have a good time and enjoy myself. I don't feel like I am working because I have a great time, but obviously there is some aspect of work to it," she said.

Pros of Being a House Manager

1. Meet new people.

2. Make new friends.

3. Have a good time.

4. Free lodging all summer.

Cons of Being a House Manager

1. Enforcing the rules.

2. Dealing with the police when too many cars are parked in the driveway or when house parties get out of control.

3. Shopping for food.

4. Playing mediator when people don't get along.

Resources

Books

How to Form a Nonprofit Corporation by Anthony Mancuso (Nolo Press, January 1998)

The Nonprofit Handbook; call (202)466-1234 to obtain a copy. (The Chronicle of Philanthropy in D.C.)

Travel Websites

www.cheaptickets.com

www.expedia.com

www.hotwire.com

www.orbitz.com

www.travelocity.com

www.travelzoo.com/top20. Every week it offers the very best travel deals. For example, during the week of July 25, 2001, it listed a Las Vegas package for two nights round-trip from Chicago for $159.

Now that you've created a social network from the charity scene and your travels, you should have enough new friends to start an investment club. The last chapter discusses how to do just that!

CHAPTER 15

Girlfriend: Get in the Game! Using Investment Clubs to Create Cash

The average single, urban woman is savvier with her money than women living in the country, has more long-term goals than country women, and doesn't want to be at the mercy of a man.

The sooner she plans for her future, the better off she'll be financially. She may be buying a home, getting married, or starting a business. Having an investment club can help her create a stream of income that can help her cope with all of those situations.

Single, urban women are more likely to be proactive when it comes to their finances. Women living in cities seek out other single women to bond with and for good reason: Studies show that women learn better in groups. Investment clubs are a great way to kill two birds with one stone. Women can meet with their girlfriends once a month socially and during the same meeting learn something new about investing.

If managed correctly, an investment club can give single women money to fall back on in case of emergencies, provide income for retirement, and even help women start businesses.

It's time to get in the game!

Five Ways Single, Urban Women Benefit From Investment Clubs

1. Clubs help young women to form lasting friendships in a lonely city.

2. Clubs help women to create a source of cash.

3. Clubs are a proactive way for women to empower themselves about money and in the process liberate themselves.

4. Clubs are a great way for young, single, urban women to learn about finances and the market.

5. Club members learn skills running a corporation that they can use if they ever decide to start their own business.

•••

Example

When twenty-five-year-old Leigh Ann Alsten constantly complained to her sister Sarabeth that she didn't have enough money at the end of the month to pay for her subscription to Vanity Fair, *thirty-year-old Sarabeth urged her to help start an investment club. Sarabeth and Leigh Ann put their heads together and launched the Lipstick Loot Investment Club in Dallas. Neither Leigh Ann nor Sarabeth had any clue about stocks or how to track them. Their jobs do not expose them to the financial world. Leigh Ann works in a physician's office as a managed care specialist. Sarabeth works as a buyer.*

Every day, Leigh Ann maneuvers through the heavy highway traffic in an old Volkswagen. "The Volkswagen was cool when I first graduated from college but I'm over it. Hello! All my friends are driving new Jettas and convertible Mercedes-Benzes. Sarabeth said that if we started this invest-ment club, we'd have more money to buy what we wanted," Leigh Ann said, her black leather pants glistening in the sun. "At first, I thought an investment club was some kind of gambling ring, but I went along with it because I needed money to buy a new car."

All that has changed since Leigh Ann became one of the founding members of the investment club. She has learned the basics of what makes a stock price what it is, why it goes up and down, and how a stock's sales affect what the price is going to be.

To start the club, the sisters contacted the National Association of Investment Clubs, met informally, and started to read over the guidelines that the NAIC had sent them through the mail. "The NAIC sent a representative to speak to us to give us a little more insight into how to put the group together," said Leigh Ann, fingering a lock of her blond hair. "We are constantly learning. One of our stocks just split this month. I was able to carry on a conversation with my boyfriend Brad about stock splits! He was impressed."

Prior to moving to the city, Leigh Ann said she never thought about finances. "It wasn't until I came to Dallas that I became aware of the need for women to plan for their financial futures," Leigh Ann said. "I have so much more to worry about in the city."

Once she realized the empowerment of an investment club, Leigh Ann helped recruit former college roommates, sorority sisters, and coworkers. Lipstick Loot's other eleven members are women between the ages of twenty-five and thirty-five years old, whose professions include a marketing firm executive, nurse, schoolteacher, and photographer. They meet once a month over wine and snacks in a meeting room at a local church.

"It's like totally cool. It's a great way to do that girl-bonding thing and learn something while you're at it. At the end of the meeting, we end up exchanging information about great places to get your eyebrows waxed or new singles clubs," Leigh Ann said. "I would never have needed to organize a club back in my hometown of Bandera, Texas. There just wasn't a need to be organized. But living in the city, I've had to come up with innovative ways to create cash."

Members invest $50 a month. Since its inception, the club has a total of $5,159 invested. The portfolio contains Cisco, a technology company;

Medtronics, a medical and pharmaceutical company; EMC, a data storage company; and Adobe, a publishing software company. The portfolio has shown a 9 percent return.

Leigh Ann says her confidence level has improved dramatically in the year she has been involved with Lipstick Loot. "A year ago, if I was at a work function and people started talking about investing, I wouldn't even get near the conversation because I didn't know anything about it. I just had zero knowledge. At least now I can get in a conversation and know what they are talking about and know why these stocks are going up and down," she said with a Texas twang.

Although the club hasn't earned enough money for Leigh Ann to buy her new car yet, it has helped her to become more conscious of her money. "I'll give it another two or three years and then I should probably be getting some money from the portfolio. Until then, I've found ways to cut back so that I can save for a convertible Volkswagen Cabriolet. It's really about being aware of where your money goes and I've become a lot more money-conscious since starting this club," she said.

• •

Investment clubs help women to learn about the market and become more aware of where their money is going.

Like Leigh Ann, initially many women are generally more fearful than men about investing, according to studies. But when we do learn about investing, we tend to do it better in a group setting, such as in an investment club.

According to a survey conducted in 2000 for Charles Schwab, 73 percent of men and only 52 percent of women said that investing is fun. More than half of all women (57 percent) indicated they would prefer to delegate investment management to a professional. Twice as many women (48 percent) as men (24 percent) confessed "investing is scary for me," and a majority of women (54 percent) likened investing to gambling.

The reason women are more fearful than men is a lack of knowledge. Women have been socialized not to handle the family money. Other reasons are that money and investing are not typically in a school's curriculum, money is still a taboo topic, and families are not talking about money and investing at the dinner table. As a result, traditionally it hasn't been easy for girls and women to learn about investing.

Which of the following, if any, have you ever bought either for retirement purposes or for other investing purposes?

	Men	Women
Stocks	43%	37%
Bonds	24%	30%
Money Market Funds	29%	24%
Mutual Funds	40%	33%

When Oppenheimer Funds asked women, when it comes to investing, how knowledgeable do you consider yourself?—these were the results:

Percentage	Response
7%	Very knowledgeable
45%	Somewhat knowledgeable
47%	Not very knowledgeable
1%	They didn't know

But when women do learn about it, investment clubs are a preferred way for them to expand their knowledge. Women tend to enjoy learning in a shared environment, and they tend to want to be with other women.

"We found that women want to learn in a seminar format or an investment club format. I think that is a way for women to learn a serious subject in a more fun way. You not only learn new things but you learn from each other's experiences and stories," says Carrie Schwab Pomerantz, vice president of Consumer Education with Schwab.

Women learn best with other women because they benefit from and enjoy a shared learning environment.

Terms You Can Expect to Learn in an Investment Club

1. Profitability of a company

2. Growth margins

3. Net margins

4. Long-term debt

5. Flow ratio

6. P/E ratio

7. Earnings per share

An investment club is one way that women can pool their resources to build wealth.

An investment club is a group of ten to fifteen people who get together on a monthly basis, to learn from each other, building knowledge and experience about investing and stocks. They pool their money every month, usually between $50 to $100 each, to buy stocks.

Most people who start investment clubs are people with no prior knowledge of investing, who may only have limited funds. More women are starting investment clubs than ever before. In 1990, the National Association of Investors Corporation was made up of

60 percent men and 40 percent women. In 2000, membership consisted of 60 percent women and 40 percent men. "The reasons are that there are more women entering the workforce in the past ten to fifteen years, more women having careers where they can earn a substantial income, and more women becoming single heads of households," said Jonathon Strong, manager of membership for the NAIC.

The number of investment clubs is growing. In 2000, there were 36,650 NAIC investment clubs, which is ten times the 3,642 clubs that existed in 1980. NAIC investment clubs invest an average of $928 each month in common stocks, and the average investment club is four and a half years old. Generally speaking, these clubs have done well. The average annual rate of return for all NAIC investment clubs during the twelve months ending April 2000 was 41.5 percent. The average annual rate of return for the lifetime of all NAIC clubs is 31.3 percent

Other good ways to become a club member are to join an existing one or start one with family members. When starting or joining an investment club, look for people who are interested in following a similar investing philosophy but have different career backgrounds—you don't want a club of all hairdressers or nurses. You want a club that includes people from varying backgrounds to bring new investing ideas to the table.

The advantages of an investment club are that you learn from others, your investment is much larger with the club because you are pooling money with other people, and it offers opportunities to socialize. The risks are that the stock market is volatile and you may lose your money, and investment clubs require a commitment of time.

Women find that a club takes more time than they initially envisioned, especially during the first year. With any profitable venture, the initial start-up is going to take extra time, and you need to be committed and prepared for that.

Create an investment club with people who have the same investment philosophy.

Types of investment clubs to look for include those that invest in stocks or mutual funds and those that have different investment philosophies, such as an aggressive approach or a buy-and-hold philosophy.

How to Research Stock

- Select an investing stock.
- Go to Yahoo Finance icon at *www.yahoo.com*.
- Punch in the stock's symbol.
- Check to see how much cash the company has on hand. A lot of cash means it's a worthwhile company to investigate further.
- To investigate further, call the company's investor relations department to request a copy of their annual report and other marketing material.

....

Example

Being a member of an investment club can be an avenue to prosperity. The seven members of the Cool Chicks Investment Club (CCIC) in Los Angeles have accrued $46,000 in just three years investing up to $100 a month in the stock market.

"We started thinking about retirement and we found that an investment club was a way to make money," said Stella Mott, secretary of the club.

The women in the group were all members of a college sorority at UCLA. They range in age from thirty to thirty-five. Stella started the club by following directions in a book about starting an investment club.

CCIC elected a board, which includes a president, secretary, vice president, and treasurer. Every member is a partner, with one vote on purchasing or selling stock. The girls meet once a month, alternating among each other's apartments.

Problems with certain club members have come up. Stella recalls one member who didn't contribute financially for months.

"Allison was a health counselor who was out of work. She had left her job to try to start her own business as a nutritionist, but it wasn't working out because she wasn't networking enough. We tried to overlook her lack of participation. But after months of no response, we put our foot down. I mean, we're all struggling out here," Stella said, with a frustrated look on her face.

The group amended their partnership agreement so that two missed consecutive meetings would result in termination from the partnership. "Allison has requested a leave of absence to find a job and promises to rejoin us in the next few months," Stella said.

....

Things to Think About Before Starting a Club

- Do all the members of the group have the same investing goals?

- Do you all live within half an hour's driving distance or a thirty-minute train or bus ride from one another?

- Do your personalities match? This is important because you will be pooling your money and working as a team to build wealth. If you don't get along, the club may fall apart.

- Are you all more or less equal in terms of income? You don't want to wind up with club members who can't afford to make the monthly investment.

- Do you have the time it takes to be involved in an investment club? Clubs usually meet once a month for one to three hours depending on the amount of business that needs to be handled.

••

Example

Kathy Sandrock has been a member of the Women's Investor Network (WIN) club in Akron, Ohio, for more than a year. WIN was founded three years ago by coworkers at Amer Cunningham, a law firm. It has been quite successful. For example, the group saw a 25 percent return on its investment during the second quarter of 2000.

Before getting involved in the club, Kathy said she was ignorant about investing. "I really wanted to get involved in some kind of a club because I wasn't familiar enough to go in by myself and just start picking stocks. I thought this was the best way to go," Kathy said. "We worked together so I didn't think I was going to be steered wrong. It has helped me as far as investment knowledge and what to look for and how to read different stocks and how stocks have performed over the past several months. It has made me smarter about investing."

The legal secretary says the most important skill she's learned is how to research. "You have to really do a lot of research on what you are going to invest in and kind of watch the market. You also have to rely on instinct."

••

In an investment club, there's safety in numbers.

Eight Steps to Make Starting an Investment Club Easier

1. *Contact the National Association of Investors Corp.* This is the only organization for investment clubs that can give you information on starting and running an investment club. Their website is *www.better-investing.org* or call 1-877-ASK-NAIC.

2. *Draft a mission statement.* Write out a statement detailing the club's philosophy, mission, goals, and purpose.

   For example, the mission statement of CCIC is to create a stream of income for its members by investing aggressively in stocks that have a 30 percent growth rate and to help educate children about investing as part of community service.

3. *Register your club with the county clerk's office.* This will ensure that the club's name can't be used by any other business in that county. This is important because you want to prevent being mistaken for another organization.

4. *Elect officers.* You'll need at least a president, vice president, treasurer, and secretary. The president moderates meetings, the secretary keeps minutes. The treasurer prepares the monthly financial report and year-end tax information and signs all the club's checks. The vice president conducts meetings if the president is absent.

5. *Consult with an accountant.* The accountant files Form SS-4 with the IRS to get the club an Employer Identification Number. It's important to establish a relationship early on with an accountant who can help with numbers and tax statements that must be issued every year when capital gains are realized.

6. *Draw up a partnership agreement.* The NAIC will provide you with a partnership agreement that simply asks you to fill in the blanks. This is needed to lay the ground rules for your club.

7. *Open a checking account.* The account permits the club to pay administrative fees, such as envelopes, postage, and paper to mail meeting notices. The treasurer signs checks on behalf of the club.

8. *Select a broker.* Ask friends for recommendations and conduct a background check on the broker by calling the National Association of Securities Dealers at 800-289-9999. Ask that the broker provide prospectuses and annual reports on stocks the club is interested in purchasing.

Clubs Have Staying Power

The longer an investment club stays together and invests, the more money it accumulates.

....

Example

The Ladies Like Money Group (LLMG) has amassed nearly $500,000 in twelve years investing just $100 a month collectively.

"We all have goals of achieving financial freedom, and we felt this was a way we could pull together our resources, our finances, and our learning to do that. So it is a vehicle for the members to financial freedom," said Leslie Bell, president of the club.

The ten-member LLMG only meets every other month on the third Saturday because some of the members live in other states. It's advisable that members live in close proximity to one another. However, circumstances sometimes require that members move out of state, leaving the remaining club members to work around their absence. Often clubs wind up having conference calls with out-of-state club members, and still more are using the Internet to communicate.

The absence of some members can affect the quality of the meeting because club members discuss potential stock investments. "We divide our portfolio and each member is assigned one or two companies to follow. You discuss information about the company and then everyone asks questions regarding your presentation and we vote," Leslie said. The longer a partner has been a member of the club, the more voting power she has. "I am a charter partner, so my shares are around a hundred shares, whereas someone who came in three years ago would only have about twenty shares," the petite brunette said.

The ultimate goal of LLMG is to create a stream of income with its $497,772 in assets. "Our projection is that in five years we will make a million dollars. We plan to take a third of that and invest it in real estate, a business, a franchise, or something ongoing," Leslie said. The thirty-five-year-old started the club because she wanted to retire by the time she was forty.

"Twelve years ago I was saddled with college debt, driving a very expensive, leased Mercedes. I lost my job and everything collapsed. I lost everything: my apartment, my car, my emotional sobriety," Leslie said. "It was in that dark hour that I got the idea of starting an investment club, which I had read about, so that I would at least have somewhere to go in case of an emergency."

Leslie wound up borrowing money from her parents but vowed that she would never be in that position again. "At least now I know that if I have a crisis, I can cash in my shares in the investment club and have liquidity," Leslie said. "I am grateful. An investment club isn't something I would have been exposed to in my small hometown."

. . . .

Although it's not ideal to withdraw money from your investment club portfolio, it's comforting to know that you have access to cash if you need it. It becomes inevitable to withdraw money if one of the partners leaves the club. Most investment club bylaws require that clubs pay a departing member within two months of her withdrawal request.

Politics can threaten the delicate balance of a group of women. That is especially true when it comes to elections and more than one woman wants to be president. In these cases, it's important for the club members to talk about the tension and politics that are developing rather than denying it.

Overall, investment clubs are a great way for single, urban women to form lasting friendships in what may otherwise be a cold, isolating, and lonely city.

APPENDIX

....

Resources

Salons That Offer Free or Discounted Hair Services as Part of Training

Atlanta

Bob Steele Hair Salon
4403 Northside Parkway, NW, Suite 160
404-262-9499, ext. 341
Monday is class night, when they do free haircuts and color if you're chosen as a model. Call to inquire.

Chicago

Pivot Point Int'l. Advanced Education
1791 West Howard Street
800-886-HAIR, ext. 365
Call to make an appointment. Haircuts: $5

Los Angeles Area

Vidal Sassoon Academy
321 Santa Monica Boulevard
Los Angeles
310-255-0011, ext. 1
They offer both haircuts and color; just call in to make an appointment. Haircuts: $17 during the week and $23 on Saturday.

Louis Licari Color Group
450 North Cañon Drive
Beverly Hills
310-550-9344
Classes held only one Monday each month, so book at least a month in advance. Haircuts: $25.

Fred Segal Beauty
420 Broadway
Santa Monica
866-550-1800
Leave your name and a message to join their model call. If you are willing to get a totally new style, cuts at the hair workshops are free.

New York City

Clairol Consumer Research Forum
345 Park Avenue
212-546-2772 or 212-546-2773
This organization pays you as part of research to color your hair.

Frederic Fekkai Beaute de Provence
15 East 57th Street
212-753-9500

Louis Licari
693 Fifth Avenue
212-758-2090

San Francisco

Gerard's International Advanced Haircutting Center
2519 Van Ness Avenue
415-441-1156
Free haircuts for those who are willing to let the student stylist choose their hairstyle.

Vidal Sassoon Education Centre
359 Sutter Street
415-956-9640
Come in on Friday at 6:15 to see if you fit as a model for their students. The type of haircut you get depends on what the students are working on. Haircuts: $16, cash only.

Out-of-the-Way Boutiques that Sell Designer Duds at a Discount

Chicago

Clever Alice
2248 North Clark Street
773-665-0555
This boutique always has a sale rack with up to half-price markdowns.

The Daisy Shop, Women's Couture Resale
67 East Oak Street, 6th Floor
312-943-8880
Very gently worn, both vintage and current top-end designers.

Designer Resale of Chicago Inc.
658 North Dearborn Street
312-587-3312

Los Angeles Area

The Address Boutique
1116 Wilshire Boulevard
Santa Monica
310-394-1406
"New and Resale Designer Fashions Remarkably Discounted."
Designer labels, very lightly worn, including Gucci, Prada, Armani, and Chanel. They advertise that they sell the gowns that the stars wear once or twice.

Maxfield Bleu
151 North Robertson
Los Angeles
310-275-7007
Sales annex for the Maxfield boutique. Sells clothing by most high-end European and Japanese designers at 50 to 60 percent off.

Citadel Factory Stores
5675 East Telegraph Road
Commerce
323-888-1724
Ann Taylor, BCBG, Max Azria, Nine West

The Place
8820 South Sepulveda
Los Angeles
310-645-1539
Designer resale, lightly worn, Armani, La Croix, Chanel, etc.

New York City

Aaron's
627 Fifth Avenue
Brooklyn
718-768-5400 or *www.aarons.com*
Up to 30% off designer clothes.

Luxury Brand Outlet
355 East 78th Street
212-988-5603

Zara
750 Lexington Avenue (at 59th Street)
212-754-1120
or
39 West 34th Street (at Fifth Avenue)
212-868-6551

Best Places to Shop for Bargain Clothing

Atlanta Area

Alpharetta Bargain Store
131 South Main Street
Alpharetta
770-475-5062
Great buys on designer clothing with some real finds mixed in. Be patient. There are great selections of 30,000 pieces at any one time including items for women, children, and men. You'll also find formalwear! Check out their special buy section for super deals.

Backstreet Boutique
3655 Roswell Road NW, Suite 206
Atlanta
404-262-7783
Small boutique that's big on resale designer labels and accessories.

Fantastic Finds
220 Sandy Springs Circle NW
Atlanta
404-303-1313
This boutique resells designer clothing and the top-of-the-line brands for a fashion forward yet stylish (timeless) dresser. You'll also find new items and accessories. The dedicated store owner is usually on the premises and her sense of style makes this one of the favorite resell shops for a brand shopper, plus her fashions are tip-top. She only buys the best and turns down the rest. A discriminating buyer who doesn't mind gently worn clothing will like this high-fashion boutique.

Psycho Sisters Consignment Shops
428 Moreland Avenue
Atlanta
404-523-0100
Cool clothes for cool people. This resell shop is jam-packed with current mall, club and disco trends, plus vintage everything. Great place to find funky vintage costumes as well as in-style clothing, jeans, and trendy accessories at bargain prices. This store knows their customers and there are five locations in Atlanta. An Atlanta shopping haunt if you're a consignment shopper and like far-out clothes or clothes with a flair.

Value City
1901 Terrell Mill Road, SE
Atlanta
770-951-5665
Takes time, but good buys on brand names hidden on the racks.

Source: Robyn Freedman Spizman (*www.robynspizman.com*), the Super Shopper on NBC's WXIA TV in Atlanta and coauthor of *300 Incredible Things for Women on the Internet.*

Miami Area

Aristocratica
71 Southeast First Avenue
Boca Raton
561-347-8778
A consignment boutique that features everything from corporate suits to 1980s' glam Gucci bags.

Brahams
2832 Stirling Road
Hollywood
954-925-6377

Mostly damaged clothing from stores that include Banana Republic, Express, Limited, BGBG, and Victoria's Secret. Prices max out at $14.99 for pants and $6.99 for tops and then additional markdowns are taken.

Cheap Frills
701 George Bush Boulevard
Delray Beach
561-274-2113
An odd lot of designer goods mixed in with lesser labels.

Couture and More
139 North County Road
Palm Beach
561-835-9979
A designer seconds store with an abundant selection of Michael Kors.

Church Mouse
374-378 South County Road
Palm Beach
561-659-2154
This thrift is only open during season.

Déjà Vu
219 Royal Poinciana Way
Palm Beach
561-833-6624
The resale house of Chanel. But the real deals are in the back, where retro Bill Blass, Oscar de la Renta, Gucci, and YSL are hanging out. No digging through piles here; clothes are in impeccable condition and very organized.

Designers to You
307 Royal Poinciana Way
Palm Beach
561-833-3363
Where you can find discount special occasion clothing by Carolina Herrera, Cerutti, Halston, and other couture designers. Selection is geared toward the ladies who lunch and have functions to attend.

Encore Shop
269 Giralda Avenue
Coral Gables
305-444-2660
A thrift that has a constant flow of merchandise donated by Miami's young society.

Goodwill Embassy Boutique
210 Sunset Avenue
Palm Beach
561-832-8199
A thrift where you can find Louis Vuitton bags, Stone Marten fur coats, Bruno Magli snake-skin heels, mint condition black Ferragamo bags, and Oscar de la Renta gowns—all for pennies.

Hospice Resale Shops East and South
139 North County Road
Palm Beach
561-820-0098
or
391 Belvedere Road
West Palm Beach
561-832-6649
Dig and find vintage clothing and crocodile and snake handbags.

Razamataz
555 North Federal Highway
Boca Raton
561–394–4592
This resale shop features Manolo Blahniks and couture clothing.

Shoe Bazaar
2200 Glades Road
Boca Raton
561–392–0119

Upscale Wholesale
1678 Northeast 205 Terrace
North Miami Beach
305–999–9008
Geared toward club-hopping fashionistas. Labels include Versace, D&G, Gucci, Prada, Iceberg, Fendi, Moschino, and Gianfranco Ferre. Open by appointment only.

Source: *www.TheySay.com*, a monthly newsletter and website founded by shopping authority and fashionista Karen Schlesinger.

New York City

Century 21
22 Cortlandt Street near Broadway
212–227–9092
www.century21deptstores.com

You've got to dig deep at this bargain mecca . . . but if you're up for the thrill of the hunt, you can score some serious finds at unheard-of prices. Go well-fed and with lots of energy to rummage. Deep discounts on everything from Prada to Polo, pencils to padded bras. Caveat emptor: Check to make sure items are not damaged.

Find Outlet
361 West 17th Street near Ninth Avenue
212-243-3177

or

229 Mott Street near Prince Street
212-226-5167
This is a gem of a shop. Ask for Ingrid or Ike. The edited-down selection is ever-changing, but rotating designers include Katayone Adeli, Helmut Lang, and Paige Novick—often half-off retail.

Ina
101 Thompson Street
212-334-9048
Although the staff can be less than helpful at times, this second-hand shop is worth it. Ina always has a sprawling selection of almost every designer you can imagine. We've scored many an Agnes b. find here. The prices couldn't be better.

Pearl River Mart
277 Canal Street at Broadway
212-431-4770
www.pearlriver.com
A New York staple: Chinatown residents, SoHo hipsters, and anyone with a creative take on the fashion game love this (albeit overwhelming) department store packed with everything from slippers to fans to parasols to rice cookers. Not for the faint of heart.

Transfer International
594 Broadway near Houston Street, Suite 1002
212-941-5472
www.transferintl.com
Tucked away upstairs on Broadway, Alessandro Mitrotti works the phones: he knows how to get the goods. (He's got a Rolodex filled

with models and socialites, and they know where to hand their castoffs.) Also a great resource for your man: the men's selection is great.

Source: Dany Levy, founder of DailyCandy, Inc., at *www.dailycandy.com.*

Orlando Area

Burlington Brands
4949 International Drive
Orlando
407-352-5721
Not to be confused with the Coat Factory, this carries overstocks, seconds, and clearanced merchandise of designer labels. But labels may be removed from some of the clothing.

Cidas
515 N. Park Avenue
Winter Park
407-644-5635
High-end gently worn women's clothing, including Chanel, Carolina Herrera, Givenchy, and Versace. Clothing at this consignment shop is up to 80 percent off.

Jill's Upscale Consignment
1002 East Altamonte Drive
Altamonte Springs
407-865-7055

Smarti Style
5616 International Drive
Orlando
407-370-5599
Expect 30 to 70 percent below retail prices.

Super Trading Family Wear
5070 West Colonial Drive
Orlando
407-299-5588
Career wear including ladies' suits for $39. Find bridal, prom, formalwear, pageant, evening bags, costume jewelry, headpieces, hats, and hosiery. Not designer labels but trendy fashions nonetheless. Hours are Monday to Saturday, 10 to 8.

Source: Laurie Lawrence, editor for *www.BiggerBetterBargains.com*.

San Francisco

Designer Consigner
3525 Sacramento Avenue
415-440-8664
Lightly used designer clothing, including labels like Prada and Armani.

First Chop
954 Irving Street
415-564-7030
High-end designer clothing, both resale and retail.

Jeremy's
2 South Park Street, Suite 1
415-882-4929
Lots of discounted designer goods, including Dolce and Gabbana, Armani, and Chanel. Mostly samples and fashion show outtakes, so watch for missing buttons and tiny tears.

Washington, D.C.

C-Mart
1503 Rock Spring Road
Forest Hill, Maryland
410-879-7858
cmartdisc@aol.com

Outlets, Apparel Marts, and Other Bargain Stores
Around the Country

Atlanta, Georgia Area

A.W.O.L.
3210 Roswell Road Northeast
Atlanta
404-231-3300

Hill Street Warehouse
2050 Hills Avenue Northeast
Atlanta
404-352-5001

Midtown Outlets
500 Amsterdam Avenue Northeast
770-986-0340

North Georgia Premium Outlets
800 Highway 400 South
Dawsonville
706-216-3609
35 minutes north of Atlanta.

Boston, Massachusetts Area

Wrentham Village Premium Outlets
One Premium Outlets Boulevard
508-384-0600
35 minutes south of Boston.

Chicago, Illinois Area

Outlet Malls
Gingiss Outlet
542 West Roosevelt Road
Chicago
312-347-9911

Huntley Factory Shops
11800 Factory Shops Boulevard
Huntley
847-669-9100
58 factory outlets.

Lighthouse Place Premium Outlets
601 Wabash Street
Michigan City, IN
219-879-6506
One hour east of Chicago.

Resale Shops
Adjustable Resale
2903 North Milwaukee Avenue
Chicago
773-227-4776

Dandelion
2115 North Damen Avenue
Chicago
773-862-9333

Vintage
Vintage Fiber Works
1869 North Damen Avenue
Chicago
773-862-6070

Cleveland, Ohio Area
Aurora Premium Outlets
549 South Chillicothe Road
Aurora
330-562-2000
35 minutes southeast of Cleveland.

Dallas, Texas Area
Allen Premium Outlets
820 West Stacy Road
Allen
972-678-7000
25 minutes north of Dallas.

Honolulu, Hawaii Area
Waikele Premium Outlets
94-790 Lumiaina Street
Waipahu
808-676-5656
20 minutes west of Honolulu.

Las Vegas, Nevada Area

Belz Factory Outlet World
7400 South Las Vegas Boulevard
702-896-5599

Fashion Outlet
Exit 1 in Prim, Nevada
702-874-1400

Fantastic Indoor SwapMeet
Decatur Avenue
702-877-0087

Tower of Jewels
953 East Sahara Avenue
Las Vegas
702-735-4145
Jewelry at factory prices.

Los Angeles, California Area

Apparel Marts
The California Mart
Los Angeles Street between 9th Street and Olympic, L.A.
213-630-3600

The New Mart
9th Street between Main Street and Los Angeles Street, L.A.
213-627-0671
Call and ask about their Super Sample Sales.

Santee Alley
Between Santee Street and Maple Avenue from Olympic Boulevard
to 12th Street, L.A. bargains in a bazaar-like open-air market place.

For great deals on sunglasses, hosiery, perfume, belts, and bags, shop along Main Street between Olympic Boulevard and Pico Boulevard and on Santee Street between Olympic Boulevard and 11th Street.

Outlet Malls
Camarillo Premium Outlets
740 East Ventura Boulevard
Camarillo
805-445-8520
40 minutes north of Los Angeles.

The Cooper Building
Los Angeles Street near 9th Street, L.A.
213-627-3754

Desert Hills Premium Outlets
48400 Seminole Drive
Cabazon
909-849-6641
30 minutes northwest of Palm Springs.

Minneapolis, Minnesota Area

Prime Outlets
Interstate 94 East and City Road 19, south on exit 251
651-735-9060

Medford Outlet Mall
35W South to Exit 48
507-455-4111

Outlets at Albertville
I-94 and Highway 19
763-497-1911

New Haven, Connecticut Area

Clinton Crossing Premium Outlets
20-A Killingworth Turnpike
Clinton
860–664–0700
20 minutes east of New Haven.

New York City, New York Area

Woodbury Common Premium Outlets
498 Red Apple Court
Central Valley
845–928–4000
One hour north of Manhattan.

Liberty Village Premium Outlets
One Church Street
Flemington, New Jersey
908–782–8550

Orlando, Florida

Orlando Premium Outlets
8200 Vineland Avenue
Orlando
407–238–7787
Minutes from Walt Disney World.

Sacramento, California Area

Folsom Premium Outlets
13000 Folsom Boulevard
Folsom
916–985–0312
30 minutes northeast of Sacramento.

San Diego, California Area

La Jolla Village Square
8657 Villa La Jolla Drive
La Jolla
858-455-7550

Mission Valley Center West
1100 Camino del Rio North
San Diego
619-296-6375

Nordstrom Rack
1640 Camino del Rio North
San Diego
619-296-0143

Shoe Pavilion
4240 Kearny Mesa Road
San Diego
858-492-9833

or

3337 Rosecrans Street
San Diego
619-222-6787

San Francisco, California Area

Napa Premium Outlets
629 Factory Stores Drive
Napa
707-226-9876
One hour north of San Francisco.

Petaluma Premium Outlets
2200 Petaluma Boulevard North
Petaluma
707-778-9300
50 minutes north of San Francisco.

Washington, D.C. Area

Outlet Malls

City Place Mall
8661 Colesville Road
Silver Spring, Maryland
301-589-1091

Leesburg Corner Premium Outlets
241 Fort Evans Road Northeast
Leesburg, Virginia
703-737-3071
35 minutes northwest of Washington, D.C.
www.chelseagca.com/location/leesburg/lees.html

Prime Outlets Hagerstown
495 Prime Outlets Boulevard
Hagerstown, Maryland
888-883-6288
www.primeoutlets.com

Potomac Mills
2700 Potomac Mills Circle
Near Woodbridge, Virginia
703-643-1054
www.potomacmills.com

Designer Resale Shops

Encore Resale Dress Shop
3715 Macomb Street NW
Washington, D.C.
202-966-8122

Inga's Once Is Not Enough
4830 MacArthur Boulevard NW, 2nd Floor
Washington, D.C.
202-337-3072

Second Chance
7702 Woodmont Avenue
Bethesda, Maryland
301-652-6606

Second Hand Rose
1516 Wisconsin Avenue NW
Washington, D.C.
202-337-3378

Secondi
1702 Connecticut Avenue NW
Washington, D.C.
202-667-1122

Index

and real estate agents, 51–52

renting vs. buying a, 45–46, 51

resources on buying a, 58–59

tips for buying a, 57–58

in urban areas, 46–47

Home equity loans, 157

Honolulu, outlets in, 207

Horner, Pamela, 39

House managers, 176

HOV lanes, 25

HUD (U.S. Department of
Housing and Urban
Development), 53

I

Identity theft, preventing, 148

Income:

increasing your, 18

level of, 1

of women vs. men, 12–13,
76–77

Individual Retirement Accounts
(IRAs), 157–158

"In-season" (term), 67

Insurance:

car, 7

for cell phone, 26

life, 158–160

Private Mortgage Insurance, 53

rental car, 25

Internet:

as clothes shopping resource, 72

investment information via, 19

security of finances on, 148

Investing, 113–116, 182–183

Investment club(s), 179–192

benefits of, 180, 185

definition of, 184

examples of, 180–182, 186–188,
190–191

growth of, 185

starting an, 187–190

terms used in, 184

types of, 186

IRAs, *see* Individual Retirement
Accounts

J

Janus, Sophie, 6

Job(s), 75–85. *See also*
Self-employment

changing, 83–85

disparity between men and
women on the, 76–77

finding corporate, 77

"glamour," 3

and potential for promotion,
81–83

resources on, 85–86

and salary, 77–79

and skills, 79–80

titles, job, 80–81

in urban areas vs. in small
towns, 75

Joint tenancy, 109–110

Junior boards, 164